RARE JEWEL
FOR A KING
A TRIBUTE TO KING CLANCY

RARE JEWEL
FOR A KING
A TRIBUTE TO KING CLANCY

by Anne M. Logan

foreword by Jim Coleman

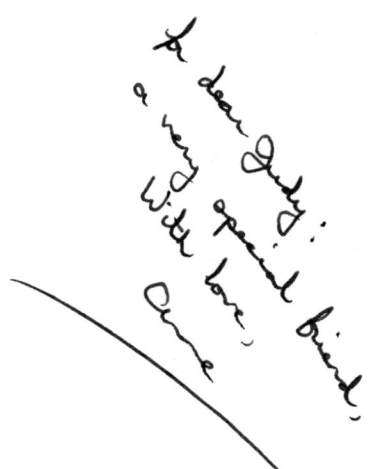

THE BOSTON MILLS PRESS

Canadian Cataloguing in Publication Data

Logan, Anne M.
 Rare jewel for a king : the story of King Clancy

Bibliography: p.
ISBN 0-919783-35-X

1. Clancy, King, 1903- 2. Hockey players – Canada - Biography. 3. Hockey coaches - Canada – Biography. 4. Toronto Maple Leafs (Hockey team) – Biography. I. Title.

GV848.5.C58L63 1986   796.96'2'0924   C86-093585-X

Copyright © Anne Logan, 1986

Published in Canada by:
THE BOSTON MILLS PRESS
132 Main Street, Erin, Ontario
N0B 1T0
(519) 833-2407

Typeset by Lexigraf, Tottenham
Printed by Ampersand, Guelph
Cover photos by Graig Abel

We wish to acknowledge the financial support and encouragement of The Canada Council, The Ontario Arts Council and The Office of the Secretary of State.

CONTENTS

9 Foreword

11 Acknowledgements

15 Ottawa

35 Rare Jewel

43 Maple Leaf Gardens

51 The Move to Toronto

61 The Thirties

77 From A Different Angle

85 Coaching

96 Photographs

129 Punch

141 A New Era

The Ottawa Citizen

Monday, January 24, 1927

The city directory shows that at 499 Clarence Street there lives a family named Clancy. The head of the household is given as Thomas Clancy, known a decade ago throughout the length and breadth of the Dominion as one of the best football players in the game at that time. In the same house lives younger "King", Frank by name, and it was this human tornado on skates who brought honour to the house of Clancy, earned an ovation the like of which has not been heard at a hockey match for ages, and carved his name deeper in its already deep niche on the scroll of hockey's famous players.

It is to this man, I dedicate this book, with respect, and with love.

Anne M. Logan

FOREWORD

Francis Michael Clancy has remained in the public eye much, much longer than any other Canadian of the twentieth century.

Since he broke into the spotlight in 1921 with the Ottawa Senators, the defending Stanley Cup champions, he has outlasted ten Canadian prime ministers and 14 governors-general of Canada.

Probably no other man in the history of our sprawling nation has enjoyed such a long, uninterrupted period of exposure to friendly public attention. King Clancy became a Canadian household name in 1921 and, as this book goes to press in 1986, his fame endures brightly.

Hockey always was a subject of consuming interest in our family. And, back in 1929, I remember my father telling a group of business friends: "If I was assembling a new professional hockey franchise — and if I was given my choice of only one player around whom to build that franchise — I'd take Frank Clancy of Ottawa."

Obviously, Conn Smythe was a gentleman who had been thinking along those same lines for some time. When Mr. Smyth decided to strengthen his burgeoning Toronto Maple Leaf operations in 1930, he bought Frank Clancy from Ottawa in what, up until that time, was the largest cash deal in the history of the National Hockey League.

King Clancy's life story isn't merely a sporting legend. He is, in fact, a legendary Canadian, a man who has become a part of our national history.

There is no other Canadian whose personal warmth has enabled him to acquire so many lasting friendships, from coast to coast. This extraordinary little man, who has bustled through life with a welcoming smile on his face and a song in his heart, has brought pleasure to everyone who had even the briefest exposure to his radiant personality.

    Anne Logan has written an affectionate biography of a man who has always deserved much affection.

Jim Coleman

ACKNOWLEDGEMENTS

I have known King Clancy since 1974 and the more I learned about him, the more I admired him. The close friendship we have formed was the inspiration for this book.

There were many people who helped me put this together and hopefully they will see evidence of their input. Harold Ballard certainly made every facility necessary available to me at Maple Leaf Gardens, and everyone there could not have been more cooperative. First, Gord Stelleck, and then his brother Bob, helped me to locate whatever I required. The girls in the hockey office even allowed me to share their birthday cake for King.

Amongst the Gardens' present board of directors, there were four members who each made significant contributions: Norman Bosworth, Donald Giffin, Paul McNamara, and Doug Roxborough.

From Clancy's playing days, there was "Red" Horner, from his refereeing days, Bill Chadwick and George Hayes, all with little anecdotes to tell, and not all of which were printable. From his coaching days I was fortunate to be assisted by Johnny Bower, Dick Duff, "Red" Kelly, Allan Stanley and Dave "Tiger" Williams, and from the present Leaf team, Jim Korn.

Through the years King has established many close associates and the most helpful amongst these were Joan Aiken, Jim Gregory, Punch Imlach, and sportswriter Milt Dunnell. At the C.B.C. I had Audrey Phillips assist me, and for the National Hockey League offices I relied on Scotty Morrison. At the Hockey Hall of Fame, Joe Romain helped locate some excellent photographs, and Graig Abel provided the cover shots. Jim Coleman, best known as a Toronto sportswriter, now in charge of the racing department at Calgary's Exhibition and Stampede, exchanged many phone calls resulting in his warm foreword.

My publisher, John Denison, was enthusiastic from Day One, and helped in many ways, not the least of which was to try and steer me away from an overly feminine viewpoint. The book had been an idea suggested to me by Phyllis and Randa Hirst, who then had to help me out with the typing. From there it went to Hilda MacMinn and Margaret McAlpin for proofreading.

All of the Clancy children contributed stories, as did his sister, Kitty Toy. It seems only fair to give a few personal asides here.

Carole Anne is married to lawyer John Kavanaugh, and they have two grown children; Karen and Stephen. Her most vivid recollection was taking the car at age fifteen, never having touched the wheel before, backing out the driveway, and going around the block, with her father in hot persuit, running behind, waving his belt! She managed to beat him home, run upstairs and lock herself in the bathroom. All he could do was yell through the door, and when she finally emerged several hours later, he was nowhere to be seen.

Judy's story concerned her husband, Bob VanLammers. They were at the dating stage when she helped him close up his family's cottage, and they arrived home rather late. King was most particular about the time his girls came home from a date so 6 a.m. would not have been acceptable! As Judy was preparing for bed, her father passed by her door. Terrified, she thought quickly, and pretended to be getting dressed for the day, and waited till he left the house before finally going to bed. The VanLammers now have two daughters themselves; Susan and Lisa.

The boys remember their dad a little differently. Tommy, having worked at O'Leary Construction with him, always admired how he used to run the bulldozers, and could operate any of the equipment to equal the best of them. He, his wife Lydia, and their two young children, Tommy and Chantal, think of King as the master story teller. When the whole family gets together at Christmas, they all sit enraptured while he regales them with his yarns. They may have heard it all before, but no one tells it like "the King".

Christmas used to be a difficult time in those days of the N.H.L. as there was always a game on the 25th, so King had to be away, be he player, referee or coach. He would phone home and each of them would talk to him in turn, and each in turn would cry. For Rae, the saddest year of all was when they brought out a new song: "I'll Be Home For Christmas".

It was not easy to grow up in the shadow of such a famous father and participate in his sport, yet Terry did so very competently. He played for Canada's Olympic team, the Leafs for a while, the Oakland Seals and three years for the Vancouver Canucks. All this was done without coaching from his father who was always away in the winter when Terry was practicing. In addition he fulfilled his mother's ambition for him by completing his college education. He is now established in the insurance business, and his wife Debby sells for an alarm systems company.

All four children think of three main characteristics about their father: his great faith, which he instilled in them, his desire for them not to drink, and the fact he never says anything bad about anyone. They also remember he was impossible to live with while he gave up smoking.

But most of all, I am indebted to the man himself, who spent countless hours reminiscing for me, and helped me in so many other ways.

I have yet to meet a person who did not like King Clancy. I have yet to meet anyone else I could say that about.

Anne M. Logan

OTTAWA

Francis Michael Clancy was born in Ottawa on February 25, 1903. Like most young boys who found their way into the National Hockey League, Francis Clancy's early years were very normal; he was born, he grew up, he laced on his first pair of skates, played shinny with the boys, and went on to sign a professional contract.

His father, Thomas Francis, had been born in Ireland, had grown up in Connecticut and moved to Canada to attend Ottawa College, becoming a successful athlete, a prominent football player, and later a coach. He was the first American import in Canadian football and went on to coach the Ottawa team of 1909 in the Eastern Football Conference and the Canadian Championship. But sports were only a past-time in those days, never a career. He taught mathematics at the University of Ottawa, where he also found time to coach their football team.

In the early days of the game, the football was "heeled," not "snapped," and Tom, excelling at this, was aptly called the "King of the Heelers.". Shortly on, this became abbreviated to "King," a nickname which remained with him the rest of his life and later was shared with his eldest son. The Clancy family, being more familiar with hearing their father called "King," still prefer to think of their brother as Frank.

Frank's mother, Catharine O'Leary, better known as Dolly, was a most graceful skater and loved to glide up and down the frozen Ottawa River. This was something her son was to take up later, in spite of the four- or five-mile walk from their home. Dolly came to love hockey so much that once, when her son received a bad gash over the eye, she leaned over the boards as he went for treatment and said to him, "Hurry back now."

A handy place to skate was a back yard rink. One day when the family was out, Clancy decided to make one in his yard, in spite of its postage-stamp size. He could not get more than a trickle from the garden hose, so he devised a better system — put the hose in the window and hook it up to the kitchen tap. This proved very successful, giving a lovely sheet of ice. There was only one problem: when he went back into the house to turn off the tap, it was not only freezing cold inside from the open door and window, he had also flooded the entire kitchen floor.

To really understand what it was like to grow up and become a hockey star fifty or sixty years ago requires some background of the sport back then. Today the players' families experience more expense and the children themselves more convenience. The first costly item today is the skates, followed by hockey equipment. Years ago they did not even know what equipment was. Today young players are driven by parents or car pools to indoor arenas to practice at a scheduled time. In Clancy's day you skated anywhere there was ice and thought nothing of walking several miles to find it, often practicing at twenty degrees below zero.

At ten or fifteen cents each, sticks were more reasonable than today's starting price of ten to fifteen dollars. There was no such thing as a goalie stick, he just used a standard one. Your first hockey stick was still a special present and Clancy's was no exception. It was to be from Santa, and it was hidden under his mother's bed. Guess who found it, could not resist trying it out and, of course, broke it. The only solution he could figure was to put the two pieces back under the bed. His poor mother was devastated when, on Christmas Eve, she went to put the presents from Santa under the tree. It was too late to buy another, so there was nothing to do but put the broken stick with the other gifts.

His Christmas skates another year were more of a success. He laced them on, stepped out the door, and slid all the way down the front steps on his behind. As if that was not bad enough, his pride was equally sore as he turned back and found his parents roaring with laughter. His next pair were a real thrill. Eddie Gerard, the star Ottawa Senators defenceman, was a friend of the senior Clancy. When he discarded his skates, he passed them along for Tom to give to his son. When Frank later joined the Big Team, paired with his hero on defence, he was still wearing the hand-me-down skates. Gerard became a friend and teacher to the young Clancy and inspired him to do likewise for other young players, one and two generations later.

There was no such thing as padding in those days. The heavy woolies and long underwear had to serve the purpose. In reality all they did was drag you down. Shin pads were the first to come, but most could not afford them. The usual protection was a magazine tied around the leg. A preference, when available, was a sweeper stick discarded from its intended use of cleaning the street car tracks.

When he was older he was taught by his school principal how to use his hockey stick as protection. Jabbing it to Clancy's stomach, the principal coached, "You're just a little fellow, so in order to take care of yourself, this thing is always the equalizer." There was many a time he did use it to protect himself, but never did he use it to intentionally injure.

For professional use, the puck was made of rubber, as it is today. For boys playing shinny without adequate protection, this hurt when it hit you, so a substitute was preferred — a frozen apple, a piece of wood, a lump of manure. Clancy had a special concoction made from gelatin, molded in a shoe polish tin and baked in the oven. It came out quite soft and smelled out the entire house.

Frank Clancy played his first organized hockey at his school, St. Joseph's, in Ottawa. Shinny on the river remained his favourite sport, but it was not what could be classified as organized. The school principal, who had never played the game himself, was Frank's only coach.

When he was too old for the school team, he joined St. Brigid's Athletic Club in the Ottawa City League. He took a while to get untracked with them, probably due to his early lack of proper coaching. His parents even asked their friend Tommy Gorman, sports editor of the *Ottawa Journal*, to give their son a few lines. He assured them he could — if Clancy ever got off the bench.

When his turn did come it was ironically because two members were caught for accepting money to play (while on another team) and lost their amateur cards. Frank took to the ice as a substitute, moving from left-wing to defence, and the team went on to win the city championship. That same year, 1919, the St. Brigid's football team was also city champion and Clancy was a member there too.

Clancy's dogged determination to win showed up in other areas. He was about to watch a five-mile road race from the sidelines when some friends hassled him about not being an entry. He decided to give it a try and wanted to do so as a representative of St. Brigid's. They would have no part of that, as their entries had all been practicing for weeks. Clancy came in third; the St. Brigid's men were also rans. At the conclusion he was congratulated on his fine performance for the club. Frank reminded them "I didn't run that race for the club. I ran unattached."

The next hockey season again saw Clancy on the bench. But finally luck prevailed when, on a road trip to Sudbury, the local brewery opened to the team for free samples. One of the members took full advantage and, as a result, did not feel much like playing hockey the next day. So the man who never touched a drop benefitted from the one who overindulged; Clancy took to the ice.

It ultimately took an injury to another team member to earn Frank a permanent place. He went on to win the scoring title for the Ottawa City League, unheard of for a defenceman. From there, he just went on and on.

The man who took Frank Clancy's career in hand was the same Irish-Canadian family friend and former sports editor, Tommy Gorman. He was now the secretary (the equivalent of today's general manager) of the Ottawa Senators hockey team and also managed the Connaught Park Race Track. He was considered jovial and capable and had the ability to always get the best out of his players. He was shrewd, and had a characteristic some called determination, others called stubbornness. Nonetheless he led four teams to Stanley Cup victories: Ottawa Senators, Chicago Black Hawks, Montreal Maroons and Montreal Canadiens. Several years later, in 1923, it was reported that "Tommy Gorman transformed Clancy from a mediocre substitute into another superstar."

King Clancy Sr. used to earn a little extra money by doing the books at the race track. Often he brought along Frank, who loved everything about the place. While his father worked, he'd wander around, watch the horses, talk to the trainers and jockeys. He started a habit which remains today as his favourite past-time, the track.

One time Gorman asked the senior Clancy specifically to bring in his son the next day as he would like to talk to him. Frank was convinced his dad knew why, but he always insisted he did not. Perhaps they wanted to hire an extra hand at the track. The real reason was a complete surprise to them all.

When he walked into the office, Frank noticed a pile of one dollar bills on the desk. Gorman told him to "practice with the club, and if you can make the team, I'll sign you for three years at $800 per season." He suggested Frank go home and talk it over with his family and come back the next day with his decision. Frank had one last question, "What is the pile of one dollar bills for?" Never having had more than fifteen cents in his pocket at any one time, it seemed like rather a lot to him. Gorman answered, "There are one hundred of them in that pile, and if you sign when you come back, I'll give them to you as a bonus."

On the way home, Frank talked it over with his father. The older Clancy, being so football-minded, was concerned that if his son signed he would have to give up other sports he enjoyed playing for fear an injury would jeopardize his career. His advice was to think it over very carefully before making a decision, a decision only he could make. Nothing more was said.

The next day Frank went in and signed the contract. He had been awake all night, not thinking about his new professional hockey status; he had visions of one hundred dollar bills floating through his head. As he put down the pen, Gorman handed him the promised bonus. With a smile a mile wide, the new Ottawa Senator headed for home.

Frank waited till dinner was well under way before he told his family what he had done. Then, with his mother's mouth still agape at the news, he added, "And Mom, I have a present for you." He put his hand in his pocket and gave her the bundle of bills. Tears still come to his eyes today as he tells that part of the story.

Now he was a pro he had to get the full rookie initiation. First they knocked him about in practice to see if he could take it. The harder they knocked, the faster he bounced back up. Then he was sent to the trainer, Cosy Dolan, for his allotment of equipment. Frank was uncertain whether to believe him or not when Cosy gave him two new sets of underwear and told him to take them home and bring his old stuff back to play in.

His first game was to be in Hamilton, and he was all set and waiting at the train station. He was dressed up like a kid for his first day of school — brand-new coat, suit, shoes, hat and tie, even a new suitcase. "What," the other players wanted to know, "was in it?" "New pyjamas, a change of underwear, shaving kit and toothbrush." They all roared. All he needed was a shaving kit.

His father had some advice for him which he still remembers. "I'd get lots of favourable publicity and some that wouldn't be so hot. If I let either the good things or the bad go to my young head, then I wasn't worth the powder to blow me off the street."

There was a whole education in his rookie experience. He was once asked by Henry Roxborough why he began his career as a defenceman, highly unusual for a man of his small stature. "There was nothing I could do about it. They wanted me on their team, and the only opening was on defence. I had to take it or leave it; and I took it." He began his career as the youngest (age 17) professional and lightest (150 lbs.) defenceman to that date.

That first game in Hamilton did not start very eventfully for Clancy; he never left the bench. Regulation time ended with the score 2-2, and in those days overtime was necessary, the tie must be broken. For some strange reason, the coach, Petey Green, elected to put Clancy and another rookie, Frank Boucher, on the ice for that shift. With sudden death a possibility, none of them could fathom it. Green thought maybe they would bring luck if nothing else, and he must have been right, as Ottawa came through for the win, although not scored by either newcomer.

It is to be remembered that the National Hockey League of 1921, when Frank Clancy became a part of it, was quite different to today's version. In the N.H.L. eastern division there were just four teams, all Canadian: Montreal, Toronto, Ottawa and Hamilton. There was also a Pacific Coast League consisting of New Westminster, Vancouver, Victoria, Portland, Spokane and Seattle, and a Western Canada Hockey League with Calgary, Saskatoon, Edmonton and Regina. Most of the arenas were outdoor with no artificial ice. A lot of people felt the real ice made for a faster game (maybe it did, you were too cold to slow down).

Ottawa was the first city to erect boards along the edge of the ice. These were originally referred to as "cushions"; not that they did much to protect the participant, it was more for the benefit of the crowd. Also hard to envision is the players cleaning and scraping the ice themselves, each team looking after their half of the rink. The game consisted then of two thirty-minute periods, so at intermission the players had to put down their sticks, replace them with scrapers and clear the surface. They did not object as much as might be expected — it helped to keep them warm by keeping moving.

The players were not as yet full-time employees of the sport. All required other occupations in order to live. Playing hockey was merely an extra part-time job. Practices were only an hour, usually in the evening, as were the games, and although the travel was time consuming, there were so few games a year it hardly affected their work. And the season only lasted from mid-December to mid-March, the season for ice.

Team members usually had a local pride to spur them on; most were native sons, playing for the city in which they had been born and raised. An added asset in Ottawa, in Clancy's valid opinion, was the support given by the Governors-General at that time, themselves not native Canadians. The Byngs were the keenest of any to hold that post, they attended every game and generally invited the team to the ballroom reception at Rideau Hall. In return, the players would send them greetings on appropriate occasions and keep them well supplied with autographed sticks. Lady Byng is now immortalized by a trophy given to the player who best exhibits skill with sportsmanlike conduct (the determining factor is total penalty minutes per season, so Clancy was never a recipient).

After their return to the Old Country, the Byngs invited several of the team — Clancy, Hec Kilrea and Alex Smith — to visit them in London. They were put up in a hotel and escorted around to all the sights by off-duty policemen. Much of the time the Byngs themselves accompanied them. As Clancy affectionately says, "We couldn't get rid of them."

With no boards or glass, the fan had ample opportunity to give a non-favoured player a good punch in the nose. It also allowed for the player to retaliate more easily. When Clancy tried it in Toronto, the fan turned out to be a plainclothes police officer. And the poor goal judge stood behind a fishing net, waving his white hankie; eventually they invented the red light.

Rules, too, were considerably different. There were not as many players on a team (six regulars and two subs) so usually one man played the entire sixty minutes. As for time, the length of a penalty was solely at the discretion of the referee; he could select one minute, two or five, depending upon how he, and he alone, viewed an infraction.

Face-offs differed from today's method, devised by referee Fred Waghorne. Previously, Waghorne would place the puck on the ice between the centremen's sticks, as in lacrosse, and then order, "Play." Invariably, before he could jump out of the way, he would be hit by flying sticks from his ankles up! One game must have particularly aggravated Waghorne, because he instructed both teams, "That's it. Rules or no rules, I'm not going to take any more of that punishment. From now on, I'm going to stand and drop the puck between your sticks. Get Ready." No one objected, so the rule was adopted.

Prior to Clancy's sojourn in the N.H.L., Stanley Cup competition was another bone of contention. Who could be eligible to compete? The one team would be the existing champion, but what qualifications were required of a challenger? Teams were popping up out of nowhere, seeking to compete for the silver rose bowl. The powers that be then decided that a challenger must be the champion team of any recognized association. One year, Ottawa, as the reigning champion, had to defend its title three times (against Winnipeg, Toronto and Brandon), all in two months.

The story is well known how this trophy was donated by Lord Stanley of Preston, a former Governor-General, and was purchased for fifty dollars. The consensus is that he would turn over in his grave if he knew it had become an emblem of professional sport; his purpose was to encourage amateur athletics, and the first name engraved on the trophy is the Montreal Amateur Athletic Association. In donating his cup, the kindly lord said, "I have for some time been thinking it would be a good thing if there were a challenge cup which could be held from year to year by the leading hockey clubs in Canada." That was in 1894. The game was played in Montreal's Victoria Rink, and it was a sold out occasion.

As Henry Roxborough described it in his book, *The Stanley Cup Story*: "In Stanley's day, hockey was mainly the sport of society. It was played as a diversion by gentlemen who had the time and means to enjoy it as a past-time. But within a few years of the Cup's presentation, the rivalries of clubs, the availability of mining money, the jealous pride of individual sponsors to prove their dollars could buy the best players — all this turned the Stanley Cup from its original lofty purpose into the arena of bitter controversy."

The amateurs and professionals both wanted the same trophy. A much more expensive cup was offered to the professionals, but the prestige was already established and there was no relenting. When the pros offered to settle the issue on the ice, the amateurs gave in. Sir H. Montague Allan, a Montreal industrialist and sports supporter, donated a trophy strictly for amateur competition, and in 1908 both the Stanley Cup and Allan Cup were competed for in their respective leagues, as they are today, almost eighty years later.

Establishing the National Hockey League as the sole owner of the prized Cup eliminated all those complications and assured only one competition a year, albeit a rather long one, but one just the same.

It was not just the status of the trophy which differed way back then. Much of the game and equipment did too. The year 1899 brought the introduction, or invention, of the first form of goal net. The design was copied from fish nets seen in Australia. Previous to its introduction, there were two upright posts. A goal occurred when the puck went between them. The judge of whether or not it did so was a goal umpire, who, on a score, would wave a white flag. The umpire's decision was final even though it was often prejudiced and impossible to prove. The net was suggested by Mr. W.R. Hewitt, then sports editor of the *Montreal Star*, and also father of the now legendary Foster Hewitt. He asked permission to attach a net between the posts for one game. The puck, caught in it, would be conclusive proof if a goal was actually scored. The idea caught on.

Although the rinks were kept to the outdoor temperature to keep the natural ice frozen, there was usually a dressing room for the team. This was the only warm spot in the arena, and those players not participating in the game preferred to sit it out there, rather than freezing on the end of the bench. At home games there was always a signal so the coach could reach them if needed, usually a buzzer — one ring for Clancy, two for Frank Boucher and three for Morley Bruce. Some of these fellows would use the time to play cards; this was not a problem. The real problem was they would also remove their skates and part of their uniforms. The coach would buzz and invariably the wrong man would appear. Not that they misunderstood their instructions; rather, it was whoever could get ready first. These shenanigans led to an N.H.L. rule change: all players must be dressed and on the bench, ready for play.

The Clancy years were certainly good ones for the Ottawa Senators. The 1921-22 season opener was December 17th, and during Frank's first home game he was knocked down by a Toronto player, a Dr. Smyllie. Tom Clancy leaned over the boards and yelled at his son, "Get up!" That night, at home, his father gave him a bit of a lecture; it was the first time he had seen his son play the game. "Son, you've got to be a little tougher to play hockey. Never let them know they hurt you." "But, Dad, sometimes I can't get up." The senior Clancy, who had much to do with forming his son's dogged determination, did not relent. "You have to get up anyway."

There was one game in which he could not get up. A notoriously rough player by the name of Sprague Cleghorn was outsmarted on a play by the Ottawa rookie. Cleghorn did not like that. He waited till the end of the period, and as the youngster was blithely skating off the ice, he called to him, "Hey, Clancy." Frank remembers turning back to answer him, and nothing more until he came to and saw a priest bending over him!

He was greeted more than favourably by the Ottawa press; for once they recognized star material. One report is amusing by today's standards, announcing "the pick of last year's City League material will go West with the Ottawas when the Senators run up against the Tigers in Jungle-Town." How far west was Jungle-Town? Hamilton, Ontario.

Before the season even began he was praised for his efforts in practice; in view of this, Gorman tore up his contract and wrote a new one with a bigger salary, saying, "Every critic around the N.H.L. circuit will soon be singing his praises."

On December 26th Frank scored his first N.H.L. goal in a game against Montreal Canadiens. The *Ottawa Citizen*, in describing the maneuver, also asserted his main talents:

> "Clancy jumped into it, fresh and determined, and grabbing a loose puck near his own goal, skated down alone. He slipped through the Canadiens defence in some way, and shot as Cleghorn and Corbeau appeared to pocket him. Vezina (the goalie) again blocked, but Clancy wriggled through the interference, shot it, scoring in sensational style. Hundreds jumped to their feet and thousands cheered themselves hoarse. They had found a new idol."

Farther on, the *Citizen* continued:

> "That the Ottawa club made a ten strike in getting Frank Clancy is now a settled fact. Young 'King' fairly electrified the spectators by his speed, stick-handling, aggressiveness and demon-like back-checking."

It is not to be thought he was an angelic performer, as another game, a 9-0 loss to Hamilton, would attest: "Clancy was the worst offender and slashed repeatedly, until he ran into Roach, who cut him down."

The season ended with Ottawa nosing out the Toronto St. Pats for first place, only to lose the semi-final Stanley Cup games back to them. At that time the series was two games, total points. Toronto won both 5-4.

Now that his première season was complete, Clancy decided to buy himself a new pair of skates. He went into Ketchums on Spark Street and told them what he wanted. The clerk, whose name he still remembers, Mr. Hensall, showed him a suitable pair but said he would have to order them in for him if that was what he wanted. Hensall had been asked to put these aside for "the new rookie sensation with the Senators, Clancy." So he left the store and never let on.

The 1922-23 season was an even better one. According to the *Ottawa Citizen* "Clancy opened the eyes of the fans by his sensational play." The sport, too, was taking off in popularity. "There were 8,000 people in the Toronto Arena Gardens when Ottawa and St. Pats collided Wednesday night. Toronto has gone frantic on pro hockey and the world's champions have had capacity houses for each of their games to date. Ottawa are the magnetic drawing card, however, all around the circuit."

Coach Green was ordered to cease using a megaphone to instruct his players, but seemed to manage without. He asserted that "Clancy is too fast and too aggressive to be kept on the bench." The owner of the Auditorium, where the games were played decided with Clancy playing regularly he "would require extra insurance against damage to the end of the arena." Perhaps that was his way to get back at King for calling the building "Ted Day's Mint." Ottawa were the N.H.L. champions that year and beat out Montreal for the Eastern final of the Stanley Cup.

"It was asking much of a hockey team to travel approximately two thousand miles from the East to the Pacific coast and play two teams of champions. The weather conditions in the East and West at this time of year are greatly different and coming from zero weather into almost summer could have a deterrent effect on the players."

For Clancy it was a thrill going west to see the Rockies. Their train car, *The Neptune*, was jammed with cases of beer, even in the ladies' room, and a piano somehow got aboard. Frank and the other teetotaler (Gerard) likely had the most fun but still were not spared any expense. They were expected to pay their share of the beer money anyway. It was more money than King had taken with him for expenses.

The first series was against the Pacific Coast League champion, the Vancouver Maroons. Ottawa won three straight games, leading Tommy Gorman to write in an article for his hometown paper:

"The present Ottawa team is the greatest hockey machine the game has ever produced. Never has a hockey team faced such terrific odds, and never has it come through in such a creditable way. Clancy skated like a flash of red, white and black lightning. The fans sat spellbound while the Ottawas absolutely humbled the Pacific Coast champions. It was hats off to Eddie Gerard and his plucky Senators."

In effect, Gorman was tipping his hat to himself, as he had assembled the team!

Now they had to play Edmonton (fortunately still in Vancouver) for the coveted Cup. It was to be a best two out of three series, and Ottawa took the first game 2-1. In the second game, Clancy played his usual role as sub, sometimes thought of as fifth wheel if there were no injuries to sub for. This was not the case here. First it was defenceman Eddie Gerard who was injured, to be replaced by Clancy. When Gerard returned, Buck Boucher went out, with Clancy taking over. Frank Nighbour was the next casualty, then Cy Denneny was cut, and finally Punch Broadbent was exhausted. Clancy filled in for them all. He had played every position in the game but one.

The goalie, Clint Benedict, was given a penalty for slashing his stick across "Bullet" Joe Simpson's knees, which at that time he had to serve himself. He threw his stick to Clancy, "Here kid, take care of this place till I get back." King looked at him questionably, "Are you crazy, god dammit?" But he picked up the stick and did as he was told. Not a goal was scored (he claims not a shot was taken either) and the record stands for the only person ever to tend goal with never a point scored against him. The Senators won the game on an early goal by Broadbent. The game win also brought the Cup their way. And the papers claimed "the hero of the series was young Clancy."

The victory brought a civic reception on their return to Ottawa, after five days on the train. "All Ottawa stopped work at eleven a.m. to be present at the Union Station and adjoining streets when the train pulled in. The players had to fight their way from the concourse to the waiting cars. The police had traffic men on every corner. The team was welcomed by the Mayor Frank Plant: 'We are glad and proud to welcome you back home after your splendid victory. Ottawa is proud of you. You have done more to advertise the city than anything else for many years.'"

What a year for Frank Clancy. His team won the Stanley Cup and he helped by playing every position on the team. The bonus money he received, $750, almost equalled his year's pay, and like his first bonus, he gave the Cup winning money to his mother. For some reason he was also elected to "store" the Cup over the summer. So he took it home and placed it in his parents' living room, where his sister Kitty remembers they never once polished it, they just used it as a catch-all for candy, gum and coins.

His next contract signed on October 29th, 1923, brought a doubling of salary to $1,500 for the season. Handwritten in the margin was "It is agreed that the Ottawa Hockey Association shall not sell, exchange or otherwise dispose of the said Frank Clancy." This was initialled by F.C. and T.P.G. (Gorman).

The 1923-24 season started off well, with Clancy still playing as a sub but somehow managing to be on the ice most of the time, and his greatest attribute showing forth: "If there are any faster players in Canada's winter past-time, they are not in the National Hockey League; but this boy's powers of endurance are being tested to the breaking point." One of Clancy's later teammates, Red Horner, remembers one game in Toronto where King did go until he literally collapsed behind the net and started to hallucinate.

Montreal sportswriters were equally laudatory: "Frank Clancy gave the greatest exhibition of speed ever seen here. King had the Canadien forwards skated to exhaustion and their defencemen baffled at times." He was starting to acquire another nickname, Man O' War, after the great racehorse.

One memorable game was Ottawa's debut in New York's new "hockey palace," Madison Square Garden. Never before had this team played in an arena seating seventeen thousand. Tommy Gorman was now with the New York Americans and anxious to beat his old team. Regulation time ended with a 0-0 tie, and it was Clancy who scored the deciding and only goal at one minute and fifteen seconds into overtime. "New York fans expected much from the Ottawa team. They had been told about the great speed of King Clancy. Now they believe it all."

In the final season game of that year, "Clancy had his shooting stick working to perfection," scoring three goals in a 7-4 victory over Hamilton. To a forward, this is not a rarity; to a defenceman, it is a real feat. The season itself did not end on such a jubilant note, as the Senators lost the N.H.L. title and the Stanley Cup to the Montreal Canadiens.

As the Twenties rolled on, hockey was becoming more and more of a popular sport. The season was lengthening, the number of games increasing, and the number of "subs" carried by each team was tripled. Luckily, Clancy was now permanently a defenceman. One sportswriter, Ed Baker, bemoaned the situation: "There's one thing the N.H.L. magnates have found out, and that is the grind of thirty-six games in the regular schedule, with its attendant many games coming one upon the other, is exacting a toll. A recent game saw the Boston Bruins "shot to pieces" as the result of a few injuries and long journeys."

The whole aura of the game was changing. Now a player had to devote more time to the game, he could not hold down another job full time, it had to become part-time. Salaries had to increase, arenas had to improve. In Clancy's case, his salary over ten years was ten times exactly what it was when he first signed.

One reason for the lengthening of the season was the introduction of artificial ice, playing surface was no longer dependent upon the weather. When first developed, it proved quite the phenomenon. "The playing surface of an artificial ice hockey rink requires careful treatment and attention — much like a shiny, bald pate. A system of electric brushes is employed, which brush the surface carefully after each skating session.

"Other implements from the North Pole Barber Shop then swing into action and give the frayed and roughened surface a shave and haircut by electricity.

"By this time the ice is fairly smooth and requires only one more operation. A machine known as the 'squeegee' rolls on the rink, which insures each crack and crevice its full share of warm water, which is sprayed on the ice." The players could now retire from their ice-sweeping duties.

"Warm water is employed because, paradoxically, it freezes faster than cold. The ammonia pipes, which automatically control the hardness of the ice, are turned on full blast, and the freezing process is completed. The surface finally is as smooth and shiny as the bald-headed row on the opening night of a girl and music show."

One assertion Clancy has always made about the sport is how much rougher it was then than it is today. Witness just one game, December 4, 1924, when Ottawa defeated Montreal 2-1 in overtime. "The first period had been only in progress a short time when Hitchman was put down and out by Morenz. It could not be seen just what kind of a job Hitch received but it was effective as the long fellow was in a daze for the remainder of the game and did not get back on the ice. He was reported to be suffering a concussion.

"In the overtime period, Frank Nighbour was crowned by someone and had to be carried off the ice. Dr. McCarthy stated that the great centre ice player had been given a severe blow.

"Also in the same overtime period, Clancy rushed in with the puck and fell after shooting, to be clipped on the head by Billy Boucher. Clancy was rather stunned, and when he arose, skated toward the offender, who jabbed him in the mouth with the butt end of his stick."

Then there was the game where the referee never showed up! This time Montreal beat Ottawa 4-1 (February 4, 1923) and needless to say the Ottawa press put full blame on the no-show official. "With the rink packed with spectators, the hottest attraction of the season nearly became a fiasco due to the failure of referee Harry Hyland to put in an appearance." Both teams were on the ice before it was even noticed.

"President Calder and officials of the two clubs scoured the arena in an attempt to find a satisfactory man. Finally, Bob Meldrum, a veteran official who had not been on skates for two seasons, was persuaded to take charge of the match. Meldrum admitted that he was not familiar with the rules and reluctantly accepted the disagreeable task. The teams soon realized he could not keep up with the play. Tripping and slashing became free and easy and Meldrum, instead of ruling the offenders off, persisted in warning them, much to the delight of the Canadiens who began to lay on the hickory at a great rate."

Through it all, Clancy's career soared. By 1925 he was classified as Ottawa's superstar, having propelled the Senators to another first-place finish. One goal description, from a game in 1927, reiterates his speed and determination.

"In a flash the flying Clancy was past him with the disc on his stick. Down along the fence he flew, breaking past the Maroon forward line. Carson tried to stop him, but Clancy literally skated over the top of him and with the puck sliding ahead of him continued on towards the corner. As Dutton came over, Clancy slipped the puck past him, and shaking the attempted body check, streaked across in front of the Montreal net. Benny started out, but he was not quick enough, and as King reached the puck, he backhanded it, kneehigh, into the net, for the only goal of the game."

November 7, 1928, marked another training camp. "King Clancy should have his greatest year. He has never appeared as big and strong and his old enthusiasm has not diminished any."

But on February 14th, George Boucher, the Senator's captain, was traded to the Montreal Maroons. At that time the captain was chosen by a secret ballot amongst the players. It was not only an honour to be selected, it was also an increase, or bonus, in salary. Needless to say, the choice was Frank Clancy.

The first game in his new role was on the road and brought a 2-1 win over the Pittsburgh Pirates. "There should be a big demand for tickets in view of the fact that Frank Clancy, one of the most popular players in Big Time hockey, if not actually the most popular, will be making his home-town debut as captain of a team that has done more to advertise the City of Ottawa, not only in Canada, but throughout the United States." With such a build-up it was fortunate they won.

March of 1929 brought the voting for the N.H.L. All-Stars, chosen by the managers of each team, excluding their own. The highest number of votes possible was nine, the highest achieved was eight, for Clancy.

Not only the captain, but the whole team were starring, maintaining their first-place position in the league. At the end of four games played of the 1929-30 season, King had five goals and three assists, and stood third in the N.H.L. scoring race. But for some reason the Senators could not sell enough seats to make money, so they reduced ticket prices from one dollar to seventy-five cents in an attempt to increase attendance.

The N.H.L. also introduced a new rule called an amendment to the forward pass, "forbidding any player on the attacking side crossing his opponents' blue line ahead of the puck." Previously players were permitted to go down and plant themselves in front of the goal, while awaiting a teammate to deliver the puck.

To clarify what is now known as the off-side, Referee-in-Chief Cooper Smeaton went to each team's training camp and explained this and other rules both by blackboard lecture and in practical instruction. The theory behind his visit was to "stress the importance of working within the law."

The effect of it all on Clancy was next to nil. The penalty box, sometimes known as the sin-bin, was other times known as the King-bin. His scoring ability was likewise unaffected by the new forward pass rule. He ended the season as the first-ever winner of the Willingdon Cup, presented by the Governor-General to the Senator with the greatest number of assists, and Clancy had tallied 23. No one knew then it was to be his swan song with the Ottawa team.

While still a Senator, but with their season complete, the

able Clancy was loaned to the Vancouver Lions for an exhibition series in their city against the Boston Bruins. The *Vancouver Province* of 1930 was highly laudatory:

> "He is the greatest hockey player in the game today. Every move on Clancy's part was the signal for a tumultuous outburst of applause. He is in the game, fighting from start to finish. There is no theatrical by-play to Clancy's work. Once that whistle blows, he forgets the crowd and all else, except that there is ice under his feet, a puck to be followed, and that he possesses a pair of super strong legs, a hockey stick, an eagle eye, and a vision that functions every second."

Boston were so impressed, he then went with them to California, where they continued their exhibition games. For these he was compared to "Ty Cobb and Babe Ruth in baseball, Bobby Jones and Walter Hogan in golf, Man 'O War on the turf, and the great Jack Dempsey in the ring, where their services as specialists in their particular branch of sport were in great demand."

RARE JEWEL

On February 15, 1927, a Toronto man by the name of Conn Smythe purchased the local National Hockey League team, the St. Patricks. A hockey devotee all his life, although his main business was sand and gravel, Smythe had a taste of the N.H.L. as manager of the New York Rangers. It was a bad experience — he was fired before a year — but it made him want to own his own team. He had been honourary (which then merely meant unpaid) coach of several Varsity teams, one an Allan Cup finalist, another year the winner. Any spare time he had was spent coaching, scouting or watching hockey. Little did he know how beneficial that would be later on.

It was not as if he was looking for a cause to unload some extra money, nothing could be farther from the truth. He was still young, with a wife and two children to look after. He just loved hockey, firmly believed Toronto could support an N.H.L. franchise, and had the bullishness to convince men who could afford to back him. Not least among these was J.P. Bickell, a lifelong bachelor who struck ore in McIntyre Mines and was always keen to a worthwhile investment.

The day Smythe purchased the team, he changed the name to the Toronto Maple Leafs. That year, the Rangers, the team he had assembled for New York, won the Stanley Cup. Smythe vowed Toronto would win it in five years, but to do so he would have to build a team from scratch.

Aside from his investment in sand and hockey, Major Smythe also dabbled in the horses (it later proved to be another sport which brought him considerable renown and success). In this field he had to learn from experience, beginning as a total novice.

He picked up one filly from a Coburg lady who gave up racing and sold off all her horses at once. Rare Jewel, said filly, cost Smythe $250. She lost every race she entered, and on her last outing, on August 8th in Hamilton, she crossed the finish line an unimpressive tenth.

The 1930 Woodbine season was set to open on Saturday, September 20th and Smythe wanted to enter Rare Jewel in the Coronation Stakes for Canadian-bred two-year-olds, a race for which she had been nominated before her birth. The trainer, W.G. (Bill) Campbell, felt it was a waste of the entry fee. The jockey, Dude Foden, thought there was some hope and convinced her owner to take the chance — he also convinced his wife to bet on another horse, the favourite, Froth Blower, owned by R.W. Cowie.

Various coincidences convinced Smythe this might be his big break in racing; he also was notoriously lucky in his gambling. The horse was number seven on the card and her pole position was eleven; seven come eleven had to be good. He took some loyal pals to the track with him — Ivan Mikailoff, the wrestling promoter, business associates Ed Bickle, Hugh Aird, Larkin Maloney and Fred Crawford — and along with Smythe, they totalled the entire wagers on Rare Jewel.

It was reportedly a typical Woodbine opening, with a crowd estimated between twelve and fifteen thousand. There were two or three showers, which settled the dust, and by the time of the Stakes race all was clear again.

According to the *Toronto Telegram*:

> "Dude Foden, had much to do with the result. He slipped his filly in on the rail at the home turn, and before Baker, on Froth Blower, realized it, he was barging out in front with Rare Jewel a couple of lengths to the good. Forth Blower set sail after her and just failed to get up. J.P. White's Roche D'or, as great an outsider as Rare Jewel, ran third. Rare Jewel won by half a length over the favourite."

Foden was later fined and given a three-day suspension for rough riding — well worth it!

The odds were 107 to 1, paying $214.40 on a $2 bet, $46.75 to place, and $19.95 to show. This totalled over twelve thousand dollars to Smythe, with $3,570 for the winner's purse and $9,372.70 for his bet. It was also the first time his blue and white colours were paraded, and it remained as the largest mutuals price paid in Canada in 1930. When he was congratulated by P.J. Mulqueen, all he could think of was: "Now we can buy Clancy. Now we are going to win the Stanley Cup."

The biggest trade in hockey was yet to be made. Toronto still needed a good defenceman and Ottawa was in financial difficulty. They let it be known their best player, Frank Clancy, was available for $35,000 which would cover their previous season's loss. The Toronto directors would allow Smythe twenty to twenty-five thousand for a purchase, but would not stretch it to thirty-five thousand. Furthermore, there was a rumour about that the only city Clancy would not consider playing for was Toronto, having maintained an on-ice feud with Hap Day.

Smythe dispatched Frank Selke to Ottawa to ask if he would ever consider playing for the Maple Leafs and King said he would "for ten thousand dollars." Clancy later remembered his first phone call from the Toronto assistant. "This is Frank Selke." "And who in 'ell may he be?"

An advertisement was then placed in the sports pages of the Toronto newspapers on Thursday October 9, 1930:

> "Fans — The Directors of the Toronto Maple Leaf Hockey Club will make their decision on Friday regarding the purchase of Frank 'King' Clancy from the Ottawa Senators. What do you think of this deal? Write the hockey club's office, 11 King Street West." Signed C. Smythe.

The ad brought an overwhelming response. The club headquarters were besieged all day with visitors, telephone calls, telegrams and over two thousand letters. All were unanimously for buying Clancy. The deal involved the cash transaction of $35,000 plus forward Eric Pettinger (valued at $5,000) and defenceman Art Smith (valued at $10,000) to go from the Toronto Maple Leafs to Ottawa Senators for Frank Clancy. When asked many years later if he was not overcome with the value he brought to Ottawa, not just in the cash but additionally the other players, Clancy's typical reply was, "Well, one of them had a broken leg anyway."

The *Ottawa Citizen* called it "the biggest player deal ever consummated by the astute manager of the Leafs and constitutes a record price ever to be paid for a player in the N.H.L." They quoted Eddie Powers, manager of the Boston Tigers, as having said, "It is a deal that has surprised the hockey world, for no one expected the Toronto club, with its small rink, to pay the price asked." Little did Powers, and many others, know what Smythe had in mind for the "Toronto club's small rink."

The Ottawa newspaper did not like to think of their team as needing money, so it is interesting to note how they commented on the transaction in another issue: "There seems to be an opinion abroad that the Ottawa club parted with Clancy to get Smith, Pettinger and cash, but the boot is on the other foot, as it was Conny Smith [sic] who parted with Smith, Pettinger and cash to get the former Ottawa native."

Yet it was in February of 1929, the year of, but some months preceding the great stock market crash, when the front page headline was "Offer to Sell Hockey Club to Ottawas." The team owner, Frank Ahearn, had made a suggestion that the Auditorium Company buy the team for $100,000 plus the season's loss (estimated then around $20,000). He intimated he had received offers as high as $300,000 for the team, but they necessitated moving elsewhere. His theory was that if the Senators remained in Ottawa, locals could buy shares giving them an even greater fan interest.

Ahearn's proposal never got off the ground and so, a year later, they sought a different scheme to relieve the debt, a player sale.

Clancy was described as "a goin' hound on skates, fearless to the nth degree, possessed of a wicked shot, and carried more above his shoulders than his ears. His great determination and his bull dog spirit have carried the Senators over many a tough spot in the N.H.L. road."

The *Toronto Globe* called him "One of the three most colourful players in the world today, along with Howie Morenz, the dynamic Canadien centre luminary, and Eddie Shore, Boston's temperamental defenceman. Opinion is divided as to which is the most effective, but the majority agree that as far as being a team leader is concerned, there is only one King Clancy.

"In Clancy Toronto gets the player they need. He will give them the strongest defence they've had in years, and he will also be the team leader, as he couldn't keep in the background under any circumstances. His duels with Eddie Shore will alone be worth the price of admission to the Arena Gardens. If there is one thing he delights in more than any other it is in bodychecking the Bruin star."

The *Telegram* rated him "among the best hockey players in the world. Many deem him the best defenceman of any, a few picking Eddie Shore as his peer. He's the hardest working defenceman, he rarely rests, going at top speed all the time he is on the ice. A brilliant rusher and a deadly shot." For all the comparisons to, and on ice confrontations with, Eddie Shore, Clancy claims, "I had no problem getting along with him off the ice."

Even Tim Daly, the Leaf trainer, raved about his new team member: "Before Clancy's purchase they sold booster tickets at half price and such. But that ended when Clancy came. What hockey player could be good enough to cost $35,000, people asked. They were curious to see for themselves and it paid off. From them on, there were no more booster tickets."

And where was the subject of all this banter? The first King heard of the trade was when he picked his father up from work. His dad was mesmerized by the newspaper. The headline was "Clancy sold to Maple Leafs." His own reaction was "What the devil! I'll go to Toronto for a few seasons and it might be fun." His dad felt similarly. "You'd better go. Toronto is going to be the best hockey town in the country." That few seasons is now over fifty-five, give or take a few in other places, and the Maple Leaf tattoo is firmly on his heart.

He felt keen to make the move "because the Leafs are a young fighting club and the Toronto fans know their hockey and take it seriously. I always get a great kick out of beating the Leafs before their home fans, as the fans stirred up a lot of fun with their cheers and jeers. I would like to play in Toronto, rather than make some American city my adopted home for the hockey season."

Before leaving Ottawa he was presented with a wristwatch from his teammates. A very sentimental man, the presentation brought tears to his eyes, and when his acceptance was complete, in a room full of husky athletes, there was not a dry eye in the house. (The watch was sadly stolen from his Toronto home a few years ago, along with his Stanley Cup ring. Harold Ballard had the ring copied as a surprise for him, but there was no sample to use to do likewise with the watch.)

His arrival in Toronto was not Clancy's first meeting with Smythe, albeit the most official one he had. The first encounter was "on ice." Smythe made a habit of sitting next to the goal judge of the enemy goal-tender, a habit present-day judges are well protected from. There was a shot from far out and the puck hit the cross-bar, whereby the goal judge raised his flag. Clancy skated by and yelled, "That was not in, god dammit." Smythe replied, "It was so in. You're blind, Clancy." "Kiss my ass" was Clancy's retort. "It's still a goal," insisted Smythe. "Kiss my ass, we'll beat you anyway" was Clancy's final comment. After the game, King was more formally introduced. Upon finding Smythe so cordial, Clancy apologized for what he had said on the ice. Smythe was already hoping someday to have him on his team. "That's all right, King. If you're in the game, you're in it all the way, with everything you've got, including your mouth."

Now it was time for serious contract negotiations between Clancy and Smythe, who travelled to Ottawa soon after the trade was official. "Right then and there I knew he was the right man for us. He didn't sit still. He jumped over the top of the bed, on top of his dresser, and all over the place." The sum of ten thousand a season had been mentioned in getting King to agree to the move. Smythe, however, was pretty shrewd as a businessman and, furthermore, he's expended the bulk of his payroll just to acquire the defenceman.

In leaving Ottawa, Clancy left behind a salary of $7,200 plus $500 for being captain. He also had a part-time job with Canada Customs, which brought in another $1,800. His description of that job is typical Clancy: "I had a good job with the preventative service of Canada Customs, even though I wasn't too sure what I was supposed to be preventing."

When they finally settled, Smythe had offered $8,500 for the season, with a bonus of $1,500 if he played well. Nothing was ever written or signed, an indication of either Clancy's trust or his naiveté. No stipulation was made as to what was meant by playing well enough to receive the bonus. By the time of the season's end, Smythe was deep into construction of his new arena and the bonus was converted to shares.

None of this money talk destroyed Clancy's old thriftiness. When he arrived in Toronto, he brought with him eight solid hickory hockey sticks which he had salvaged from his Ottawa club. "What's more, I had the same eight sticks at the end of the season."

As Smythe said later to Scott Young, "I never had any trouble with Clancy about money in my life. He was the most amateur athlete I ever had. Just loved to play, and that's what Rare Jewel did for me."

MAPLE LEAF GARDENS

Smythe now had put together the team he felt could win him the Stanley Cup. The only two players remaining from the previous St. Pat's team were Irvin "Ace" Bailey and Clarence "Hap" Day.

Bailey's career was tragically cut short, and it is for this unfortunate incident that he is best remembered today. That is not as it should be. He began his career in Bracebridge as a goaltender. When almost decapitated by a blistering shot, he decided to switch positions. He also concentrated more on his other sport, lacrosse. In the fall of 1925, as a member of the Peterborough Petes, his scoring was a substantial part of what made that team the Ontario Hockey champion.

Bailey's first professional offer came from the Montreal Maroons, but Toronto topped their offer at $2,000 a season. Rather than sign Toronto's contract, he hired his own lawyer to draw one up for him. Once in the office, both were on the table; he picked up the Leaf's and signed it. Always a fast skater and a neat combination player, he reached the top in 1925-26 by leading the league in scoring.

Along with Bailey, Smythe kept Clarence Day, who had signed while a student of pharmacy at the University of Toronto in 1924, provided he would not miss any lectures. He did obtain his degree, and eventually a drug store was opened in his name where the Maple Leaf Gardens staff coffee shop is today. Day was also a stockholder and second-in-command at C. Smythe Sand Company.

"Hap" Day was the unanimous choice of the players as their captain. His coach, Art Duncan, described him:

"Happy Day is the ideal professional athlete. He is always

first to bed and first to get up when on the road. He is a born leader and admired by all his mates. Happy is a gentleman off and on the ice and a great example to the younger players. Despite seven years in pro hockey I have always found Happy willing to accept advice and anxious to cooperate in anything that is necessary for the welfare of the club."

As for Clancy's opinion: "Hap Day is the best defenceman I have had for a partner." The feeling was mutual: "I have a partner in King Clancy who knows all about his side of the rink, and I have more time to improve my own game."

To this foundation, Smythe added the famous KID line: Joe Primeau, Harvey "Busher" Jackson and Charlie Conacher, likely the most famous combination ever put together in hockey.

Primeau remains a close friend to Clancy but Conacher became his lifelong buddy. Charlie dreamed of becoming a hockey star like his older brother Lionel and used to carry out the sticks for the New York Americans whenever they were in town; he hoped to be noticed. Eventually he made the Marlboroughs, and when the team of 1928-29 won the Junior Amateur hockey championship, the Leafs eyed not only Charlie but also Jackson, Red Horner and Eddie Convey. Conacher went on to become one of Toronto's most brilliant right-wingers. But according to Horner, he still used the threat of joining his brother in New York whenever he wanted a raise in contract.

Smythe also discovered in his scouting a defenceman named George "Red" Horner. The week before Christmas, Red had played for his team at work on Friday night, Saturday afternoon he played his usual spot with the Marlies, and after that game he was approached by Smythe. "How would you like to play tonight?" Red asked where and why and was told he'd be paid $2,500 if he would sign a contract. At that time of year, and earning only $25 a week at the stock exchange, it was an offer he could not refuse, and so he played his third game in less than twenty-four hours, but this time in a Leaf uniform.

Perhaps because he was the youngest on the team, Smythe took a particular interest in Horner. At season's end he advised him to build himself up over the summer. Without the benefit of today's gyms, Red did the next best thing; he contacted a friend who ran a boys' camp north of Sudbury and applied for the job of counsellor. He was hired for $200 a month. Smythe checked on him closer to the summer and asked if he was taking his advice. Horner told him he had a chance to be a camp counsellor but could not afford to give up his other job for the summer. Smythe compensated, also paying him $200 a month, and ended up sending his own son, Stafford, as a camper.

With the accumulation of a respectable team of players, including Harold Cotton, who also worked as a car salesman and whom Clancy calls a "keen competitor," and Lorne Chabot, the goalie Smythe had so enthusiastically signed for New York, Smythe's vision broadened. The year was 1931, the world was still reeling from the effects of the Depression. No one who has not lived through this period can realize the complete emotional devastation. Labourers were starving; there was no such thing as construction. Bread lines were a mile long and every spare hand was needed in the soup kitchens. Contrary to modern-day depressions, even the wealthy were affected. People with children in private schools had to withdraw them because they could not afford the tuition; travellers had to return from holidays; mansions went up for sale at bargain prices; in New York, the stockbrokers were jumping out windows and off bridges.

None of this would stop Conn Smythe from realizing his other dream, to build a new arena. They were able to sell most of the tickets for any hockey game at the 8,000-seat Arena Gardens — later called the Mutual Street Arena and now the Terrace, specializing in roller skating. Why not build a beautiful new rink to seat 12,000 or more? They could charge more in admission, which would become increasingly necessary as years went by and player salaries increased.

As Tim Daly described the old Arena Gardens "It was more like a barn. The box seats were planks. The construction of the players' benches was just tongue and groove."

Smythe wanted a place "where people can go in evening clothes, if they want to come there from a party or dinner. We need everything new and clean, a place that people can be proud to take their wives or girlfriends to." He wanted to compete with theatres and make hockey a social attraction.

When the first announcement reached the press on January 17, 1931, it was not certain what the location would be. "The directors are considering two sites, one on College Street, and the other the Fleet Street property between Yonge and Bay streets" (now Toronto's main Post Office and Canada Customs building). "While the Leafs were in New York, Boston and other American centres, Smythe interviewed several prominent building engineers and has gathered a pretty good idea of what would fill the bill here." The Detroit Olympia style of construction was reported to be favoured by him; no balconies or posts, one long layer of seats all around.

Smythe knew it would cost at least a million dollars, perhaps closer to one and a half million. But he had some good friends and staunch supporters, two being Larkin Maloney of Canada Building Materials and J.P. Bickell, a mining magnate whom Smythe called "the best businessman I ever knew in Canada," who had "a liking for my way of doing things."

Smythe was still under criticism for his extravagance in the purchase of Clancy. "The governors of the N.H.L. insisted Conn Smythe was foolish in making such a deal. It shocked the hockey world. It sets a bad precedent." He felt they would have made the same deal if they could.

Fighting fire with fire, the major stood his ground well. "If they want to have a hockey war, we'll fight them with one of the best rinks that money can erect. Frank Clancy was the first player to come here under our 'a greater team for Toronto plan' and if things come out as expected we will have a team and arena here that will thrill the local fans."

With the support of Sun Life, who considered it a good investment, and the Canadian Bank of Commerce, Maple Leaf Gardens was incorporated on February 24, 1931, and the construction began on what was then, and remains today, Toronto's most controversial building.

The College Street site was settled upon and purchased from the T. Eaton Company, who had just opened a large store barely a block away. They preferred to part with another parcel of land a block north, but Conn Smythe was very persuasive. He convinced the head man, J.J. Vaughan, that the new arena would draw all sorts of new customers because they would have to walk by the store's windows. Vaughan not only relented, Eaton's bought shares. Once the ground was levelled, a watchman was hired (what possessed him to employ someone to guard vacant land, Smythe later wondered himself). But the Gardens was now his baby. There were countless labour pains before it was born. There were times it appeared unable to survive. But on June 1st the construction began, and five months later, on November 12th, it opened, as Smythe told Scott Young, "pretty much as I had imagined in my rosiest dreams."

The most famous setback occurred when there was no more money in the till, no more possible sources to draw from, and Sun Life had even threatened to pull out. Frank Selke, Smythe's able assistant, devised an idea. Why not convince the labourers to take twenty percent of their pay in stock certificates. In this time of vast unemployment, this project was providing work for 1,300 people. Selke was a member of the electricians union, so he became spokesman at a union meeting. Such a scheme had never been attempted before; the workers were hesitant, until considering it was that or nothing, and they took the gamble and carried on.

That agreement was the turning point for the Gardens. Smythe was able to report back to Sir John Aird at the bank, who was delighted and volunteered, "In that case, our bank will pick up the rest." Smythe was always considered to be the mastermind behind this enormous project, and a man not usually known for his humility. However, he credits the actual success to the union men who made the decision to settle for stock, and Sir John Aird "for picking up the rest."

The building was to be some 30,000 cubic feet, with seating capacity for 12,473 and standing room for 3,000. From the tip of the roof to the ice surface is 140 feet, and the $\frac{3}{4}$-to-$\frac{7}{8}$-inch-thick ice took ten hours to remove and replace, and required ten miles of piping. The bricks, placed end to end, would stretch twenty-three miles, and the entire building was fireproofed.

There are not many who know that there is also a fully equipped bowling alley upstairs, which at one time could be used by the public, but is now just empty space.

Lou Marsh, sports editor of the *Toronto Star*, joked before opening that "things are so high hat around the new Gardens that the peanut men will only be allowed to sell salted almonds." He added that "it isn't in the books for the Leafs to be beaten in their first home game in their new ice palace, t'wouldn't be policy. They had the same idea down around New York the time they inaugurated pro hockey in Madison Square Garden. After a most impressive ceremonial, the Canadiens proceeded to lambaste the daylights out of the Amerks. I know, because I was the referee."

A tradition began with the opening of Maple Leaf Gardens that continues each season: The directors are in black tie, the 48th Highlanders march on the ice playing "Road To The Isles" and the Leafs invariably lose! In this case, the Chicago Black Hawks beat them 2-1. Marsh was not sympathetic: "I'll bet Conny Smythe is glad Leafs got that game out of their systems. That should take down some of the swelled heads." W.A. Hewitt put it rather differently, "The importance of the occasion was so impressed on the minds of the Maple Leaf players that they became over-anxious and did not get together on their team play."

Hewitt was, however, most enthused with the arena: "Everybody expressed amazement and pleasure at its spaciousness, its tremendous capacity, its comfort, its beautiful colour scheme, and its adaptability for hockey with the spectators right on top of the play."

There is still one game considered the most famous ever to take place there. It was in the playoffs of 1933, on April 3rd, between Toronto and Boston. Regulation time ended in a scoreless tie, and the rule for playoffs was, and still is, that the teams must play to a win. It is a minor miracle this event has never been repeated. In the 4th period of overtime, past midnight on the time clock, Clancy scored, but the whistle had already been blown. There was no dispute; Clancy did not get the point, but no one had the reserve energy to argue. I know of one fan who gave up his seat to a lady in standing room, figuring it could not last too long, only to have to stand himself for hours. Other patrons gave up and went home, their places being taken by those following on the radio, who got in their cars and drove down — Smythe had opened the doors to let them in for free.

Finally, in the 6th overtime period, at minute five, Ken Doraty of the Leafs took a pass from Andy Blair and put the puck past Bruin goalie, Tiny Thompson. At 1:50 a.m., the Leafs had won 1-0. They played dismally the next night in New York and went on to let New York win the Stanley Cup. They never quite recovered from that game.

The Leaf coach, Dick Irvin, gave a marvelous description of sudden death overtime: "When your team gets the goal, it's sudden; but when your opponent gets it, it's death!"

Many years later, recollection of the incident prompted Clancy to comment on a real truism of hockey: "The one who makes the headlines is frequently an average player who becomes hot. All season, he [Doraty] scored a total of about five goals. Then, after more than one hundred and sixty minutes of play, he fired the shot that ended it all."

The Move To Toronto

King's first year in Toronto was prior to the building of the Gardens. It was around the time of his purchase that Smythe began his twofold task, rebuilding the Maple Leafs and building an arena around them. The team could not have done much worse than the 1930-31 season. Clancy was paid his bonus of $1,500 anyway, not in cash but in Gardens stock, and he has yet to sell those shares — a very shrewd investment.

Clancy met all his new teammates at training camp in Parry Sound. He was considerably nervous about his first encounter with such great names as Conacher, Primeau, Chabot and Day, and he was distressed to be a late arrival for camp due to his job at Customs.

Once King appeared on the scene, he was given a warm greeting by each player individually. He was then honoured at a breakfast where Hap Day, as captain, delivered a short message of welcome and expressed the hope they would all enjoy a good season. Clancy had been working out while still in Ottawa, so they were pleased to see him able to keep up to everyone else in the drills.

He was concerned how they would react to a teetotaler, not a common attribute in sport. The Ottawa club had become used to that, and the goalie had taken full advantage of it. After a game they usually passed a bottle of their favourite medicine around the dressing room. To make up for Clancy not taking a swig, Clint Benedict figured he was entitled to two. It turned out that Clancy found himself in good company; Smythe was a teetotaler and frowned on liquor in the dressing room, with the sole exception being champagne in the Stanley Cup. Hap Day also abstained, as did the coach of later years, Dick Irvin. Some of the others more than compensated.

King nearly didn't get past training camp. There was no ice yet in Parry Sound, so they were all "supposed to do a lot of walkin' and runnin' and ended up huntin' partridges in the bush. I'm walking with Chabot, and Busher Jackson is behind us. A bird flies up and Jackson puts a hole right through my hat. I never saw Chabot so mad. Me, I'm so scared I can't even speak."

Many of the team became King's lifelong friends, and he is quoted many years later as saying, "These are fellows I might never have met if I'd stayed in Ottawa, and I think I'm a better man for having met people of this calibre."

On the road trip for King's first Leaf game, he roomed with Hap Day. The routine — as for many even now — was for a steak in the early afternoon, then a nap before the game. Clancy set the alarm and dozed off. When he awoke, the phone was ringing. It was Day, downstairs, complaining that everyone was down there waiting for him. Clancy checked his watch, and sure enough, it was 7 p.m. He flew into his clothes and finished doing up his tie on the elevator. As he stepped out into the lobby, the whole team was there all right, roaring with laughter. He looked up at the clock — 5 p.m.

This was the same Hap Day whom Smythe had reservations about concerning Clancy. They had such a bitter rivalry when they were on opposing teams, would they ever adjust to being teammates? Clancy assured Smythe that it was all just a part of the game and he had the utmost respect for Day. (For those few moments after he alighted from the elevator, he may have had second thoughts!) By 1932 they had become such close friends that King was best man at Day's wedding. Hockey had become such an item by then, there was a crowd of 3,000 outside the church.

Day was also noted for his driving skills. In Winnipeg, he and Clancy were driving along at a great speed. The car in front was Foster Hewitt's, Hewitt unaware of who was behind him. The police stopped Day and warned him that he had been speeding. As Day looked ahead, he spotted that Foster had stopped by the side of the road for an emergency call. Immediately, Day looked at the officer of the law and said, "Sir, we may be speeding, but that man ahead is exposing himself in public." The policeman looked, jumped in his cruiser and stopped by Foster's car. As he was making his arrest, Day and Clancy drove by, honked and waved.

Another time, they were driving Smythe home from an out-of-town game. Day and Clancy presumed the boss was asleep, as he was curled up under a blanket in the back seat, unusually quiet. Day then figured it would be all right to drive in his usual fashion, fast. The dozing passenger could sense what was happening and piped up, "King, has anyone ever gone over Niagara Falls alive, in an Oldsmobile?"

Yet another time, Lionel Conacher helped Day in a prank. Clancy had been boasting about what a marvelous physique he had; it more than compensated for his small size, and he was so fast he didn't need a huge build like they both had. They decided they had heard enough of his bragging and would put him on display for all to see. They picked him up, in only his underwear, put him out on the hotel balcony and locked the door.

In Boston, Day decided he wanted to make a little petty cash on the side. He planned a jump in the hotel pool, fully clothed, hat, coat and all, but it would cost a dollar to watch him do it. They all paid, Red Horner took the tickets, and Day made an easy profit.

In Kitchener for an exhibition game, Clancy and Day couldn't let Halloween go by without a little trick, no treat. They snuck into all the players' rooms, tied all their clothes in knots and generally made a mess of things. Although proclaiming innocence, Clancy locked himself in his room. He could hear everyone outside trying to get at him, but he was going to out-wait them. When all was quiet, he presumed they had given up, so he opened the door and got soaked with a bucket of water.

Bob Hesketh, then a sportswriter rather than a broadcaster, later commented on such antics: "Those were uninhibited days and they were uninhibited hockey players in an uninhibited system. It has changed now, but it used to be that men were trusted to know between fun and games and work. When they felt the natural urge to blow off steam, they did, and often quite neatly. There were cast iron friendships between men who understood each other and worked better because of it."

Exhibition games, such as that played in Kitchener, until the 1960's, were not an object of profit. They were also not played with any other team. Rather, they were more like a practice session; in the case of the Leafs, it was the blue team versus the white team. But their real reasons for existence were to raise money for charity and to take the team to arenas in cities or towns other than Toronto, giving the local citizens an opportunity, which they would not otherwise have, to watch their heroes perform in person instead of just on radio or television. They would often play every night of the week, each time in a different place.

The opening game of Clancy's first season in Toronto brought plaudits from the press. J.F. Fitzgerald of the *Telegram* commented, "It looks as though the advent of King Clancy has done a lot more for the Leafs than put a star player on the ice. Always the battler, and the son of a battler, Clancy has instilled into his teammates the fighting, never-say-die spirit and that sort of thing, once rubbed in, becomes a habit, a useful, inspiring one."

Within a week, his old teammates were in town to oppose the Leafs. "Yet one noticed that Ottawa lacked something that had made them a stand-out here in the past. What Ottawa lacked, the Leafs possessed. A little battling Irishman by the name of Frank 'King' Clancy was that difference, and what a difference it proved to be. Ottawa played wonderful hockey, yet they seemed to lack that inspiration they always found in King Clancy."

The junior Clancy had no bitter feelings about the trade. As Mr. Ahearn (who had taken over from Tommy Gorman in Ottawa) assured him, it was with great regret that they let him go. He had been their only source to repay what the team had lost the year before.

His first game back in the old hometown was a thrill for him, but a real trauma for his father, who never attended another game in the Ottawa Auditorium; he would drive instead to Montreal and watch his son play there.

When he stepped on the Auditorium ice he was applauded; but from the moment he touched the puck in his new uniform, he was booed. He knew this acknowledgement was flattering and therefore he came to enjoy it. His father found it agonizing that after nine years of faithful service to the Ottawa club and fans, his son should be so maligned instead of praised. There was no way Frank could convince his dad this was the way it was in hockey. He understood, but not when it applied to his son!

The Leafs were not destined to be league champions that year, but they did make the playoffs, and one of the most important games late in the season to get them there was also one of Clancy's best. The headline of the *Toronto Telegram* read:

"Babe Ruth Of Pro Hockey Aids Leafs in 5-2 Victory" over New York Rangers. "Clancy stood out as the best player on the ice. He was on the warpath in this game and his part in the scoring of four Toronto goals during the last period was a treat to watch. The Leafs rallied to Clancy's war cry and followed the greatest defence player of modern professional hockey on a merry hunt for goals."

The year 1931-32 was a big one, led off by the opening of the new arena. Training camp was moved closer to home, where artificial ice was available (the real thing was too unreliable so early in the year). The location was St. Catharines because it also provided good hotel accommodation, easy access to Niagara Falls, a golf course and mineral baths.

Art Duncan began the season as coach, but after their miserable start, he was soon fired. The conclusion was that he had been a marvelous player but, as is often the case, made a lousy teacher. Dick Irvin was then hired, having made his mark playing for the Winnipeg Monarchs in Allan Cup play and later proving his ability as coach with the Chicago Black Hawks.

The only setback of the year was a fire in the Gardens not two months after opening. The damage was mainly to the dock and wiring, amounting to some $50,000, and the cause was believed to be welding by acetylene torch. It must also have ignited the team that year, because they went on to beat the New York Rangers in three straight games and to capture Smythe's dream, the Stanley Cup, exactly according to his prediction of five years.

Again, much of the credit was given to Clancy. To quote sportswriter (and former athlete himself) Lou Marsh, "If there was one place the Leafs stood out it was on defence. King Clancy sparkled all night. The Mighty Man from Ottawa, just a wan drawn shadow of the sturdy warrior who started out last November for the Leafs, laid into every Ranger attacker who came roaring down his side of the defensive end."

There was one manoeuvre for which King was particularly noted in his playing. Developed from his small size but great speed, it became known as the recoil check. To start, he would dig himself in on the blue line, pick out the largest opponent who was approaching the fastest, and throw himself into the air. "When the bodies crash, the puck carrier is often knocked momentarily off his stride. Clancy is always knocked momentarily, or longer, into mid-air but when he lights, he is invariably still on the inside of the rubber or at least near enough the net to clear the rebound." According to George Hainsworth, the Leaf goalie, it was not always successful, for there were times he had to clear both the puck and Clancy!

The press did not always praise Clancy. Sometimes they had fun with him too. One such occasion came as the result of an advertisement he had agreed to lend his name to. Lou Marsh just could not resist: "And now the secret of King's verdant youth is out. Always careful in his mode of living and a man of exemplary habits, it will be noted that he long ago realized that an athlete, like Napoleon's army more than a century ago, fights on his stomach. And so it is that Frank Clancy is a living, driving, speeding atom of energy because he has long been a devotee of Eno's Fruit Salts."

A rivalry developed, while playing for Toronto, between himself and Eddie Shore. On ice they vowed to kill! It has been said that nobody could get along with Shore, even off the ice. But true to form, "never saying anything against anyone," Clancy claims he always "got along with him just fine."

In one game in Boston, the Bruins were ahead 4-1. Shore got the puck and headed towards the goalie, George Hainsworth. Clancy tripped him. An irate Shore bounced up and cross-checked Clancy into the boards. The little fellow had had enough, so he up and tackled Shore, only to get punched in the face and knocked flat to the ice, having to be rescued, as per usual, by Charlie Conacher.

On another occasion, Clancy successfully tripped Shore, who raised his gloved hand all ready to punch, when the little fellow grabbed Shore's hand, shook it, and said, "How are you tonight?" Not thinking quite as fast, Shore replied, "I'm pretty good, and how are — ?"

One year in the playoffs, Shore got a minor penalty. Clancy skated by him and attempted to console him that it was quite unfair and undeserved, and he should not let the referee get away with such a call. Shore agreed, of course, and on his way to the penalty box took the puck and shot it right at the referee, Odie Cleghorn. Cleghorn responded with a ten-minute misconduct, and while Shore was off, the Leafs got the impetus they needed, tied up the game and then went on to win; a win generally credited to Clancy's quick verbiage.

One game in Boston, Shore took to the ice with a gold dressing gown (the team's colour) over his uniform. As he skated around in the pre-game warm-up it floated dramatically behind him and was a great crowd pleaser. Clancy moved to centre ice, where he could razz him a bit. "The first time you come down the ice, take care you don't get your skates tangled up in it, because knowing you, you'll fall into the end of the fence and start crying for a penalty." Shore glared, "Clancy, I'll kill you tonight." Fearlessly, the King responded, "Well, that's what I'm here for."

The most famous Eddie Shore incident is also the most tragic. It finished one man's career and certainly tarnished another. It happened in Boston on December 12, 1933. Initially, it was Clancy who had tripped Shore and sent him flying. Enraged, when he got to his feet, he charged and dumped the first blue and white sweater he could find. It happened to be Ace Bailey, who fell to the ice and lay motionless from a fractured skull.

Smythe was livid and intimated to Charlie Conacher, a giant of an athlete, that revenge was in order. Before Charlie got to the scene, Red Horner had done the deed, and Shore too lay bleeding on the ice from a broken nose. To add insult to injury, Smythe was attempting to reach Ace on the stretcher when a fan yelled at him, "Fake." This was more aggravation than the Leaf owner could stand, so he punched the fan in the face, broke his nose, and was promptly arrested. This delayed his trip to see Bailey in the hospital even further, until 2:30 in the morning.

It was ten days and two major operations before they knew if Bailey would live, and the same time for Smythe's trial to be settled. The judge was sympathetic to the circumstances and let him off with a fine.

Bailey's fortunate recovery precipitated the first ever All-Star game, which was to be a benefit to raise money for the now careerless Ace. The date was February 14 (St. Valentine's Day), 1934. The Leafs were to play a team of All-Stars, one of whom was Eddie Shore. Prior to the game, the crowd was silent, waiting to see how Shore and Bailey would react to each other. In a very dramatic moment, which brought tears to many, Shore went over to the frail Bailey and offered his hand. Bailey took it and then they embraced. Bailey never once had, nor has he to this day, claimed anything other than that it was an accident.

The rivalry existed not just between Eddie Shore and King Clancy, but a more bitter feud had developed between Art Ross, the manager of Boston, and Conn Smythe. Near the end of Clancy's first season as a Leaf, he more than redeemed himself in the eyes of his owner by outsmarting a certain referee by the name of Ion, noted for favouring Boston.

To abbreviate the *Toronto Telegram*'s rather sarcastic report, "Somebody in the N.H.L. actually outguessed 'his nibs' Sir Michael Ion, who is trying to win the title as the worst referee on Mr. Calder's staff."

It is to be remembered that in those days there was no linesman, rather, two referees. In this case the other official was a Bill Shaver, who lived in Boston. "Maple Leafs had scored three early goals and their consistent checking and rushing had Ross nearly crazy. A sensational rally by the Bruins tied the score for the home-towners . . . Lorne Chabot saved the game time and again for the Leafs with his wonderful work in goal."

Halfway through overtime, Boston scored, but our hero was

off-side. "Then King Clancy sprang an idea that was worth every dollar spent to secure his services from Ottawa. Clancy skated over to Shaver and stated he was off-side when the puck was faced off, claiming that Ion was so anxious to let the Bruins get under way again, he neglected to give 'King' time to get back into his proper position.

"Shaver had seen this to be a fact and so skated over to Ion and ordered another face-off. Ion was knocked off his feet. He just stood there, and despite manager Art Ross' firy protest, did nothing about it. He was beaten at his own game and to Clancy goes the credit."

In 1932 the battle continued. On December 14th, during a game in Boston (which the Bruins won 5-1), Red Horner and the Bruins' Joe Lamb were penalized for high-sticking. Both teams gathered around the penalty box. When the announcement was made that Horner's penalty was a minor and Lamb's was a major, Art Ross was irate and questioned the referee. It was reported in the papers that Clancy swung at Ross and the police and ushers were required to break up the melee.

The press, it turned out, were wrong, as the referee clearly witnessed that it had been Art Ross who swung at Clancy. Smythe reported Ross to the N.H.L. for hopeful disciplinary action, but none was ever taken. Smythe wasn't finished! He knew that Ross had a serious problem with hemorrhoids, so he ordered a bouquet of very long stemmed red roses, noted for their thorns, and had Clancy skate over and deliver them to Ross, with the attached card, "Stick these up your ass!"

The supreme revenge would have been to win the Stanley Cup, but that was not in the cards for the Leafs that year. They did end the season in first place, but the silver trophy went to New York.

The Thirties

When Frank Clancy moved to Toronto he was still very much the bachelor. His sisters kidded that he had many girlfriends, who changed so fast it was impossible to get to know any of them. When he first arrived he shared a suite in the Royal York Hotel with Frank Finnegan, at the rate of $1.11 a day. In 1978 Finnegan told sportswriter Al Abel of his memories of this.

"King had his car, he'd have a girlfriend, so I'd get in the back seat and we'd drive the girl home; then we'd go out and have some fun. Mind you, we didn't do anything wild in those days. Living in a hotel, you never knew who'd be sitting in the lobby to say, 'There's Clancy and Finnegan and it's 5 a.m.' Conn Smythe always reminded us that there was a train waiting to take us to the minors."

He continued,

"He always had a lot to say, good gibberish, lots of fun. We certainly had a good time. We never talked about our future, what would happen to us after we finished hockey."

Finnegan later ran a hotel with his sons in Shawville, Quebec.

Then one day, a Toronto hockey nut and friend of Hap Day's, Sam Shefsky, told Clancy he had a lovely girl he would like him to meet, Rachael Marion Watt. Two years later, on October 7, 1933, Rae, as she was better known, became Mrs. F.M. Clancy. They had a harmonious marriage for over forty years, until her death from cancer in 1977; a loss from which he has never completely recovered. "She was the greatest person God could ever give a man. One in a million. I just can't say too much about her."

Above all his other traits, King has always been known as a devoted husband and father. He adored Rae. He totally credits her with the successful upbringing of their four children, Carole Anne, Judy, Tommy and Terry. "She did a grand job, the biggest job of all. She allowed me to love hockey and be with it."

They would have seemed an unlikely couple to anyone less astute than Shefsky. The big hockey hero, recognized everywhere he went, and the little smalltown girl who admittedly didn't know a thing about hockey, let alone the players. This may have been part of the attraction.

Rae later told a Toronto writer, Margaret Scott, "King probably wondered how I could have gone through life without seeing his name in the papers and remembering it. I often look back in wonderment at how I fell in with his ways. We were an unlikely twosome. He was Irish, Catholic and gregarious. I was quiet, Scottish and Protestant.

"I found him exciting. That's what attracted me. I had never been to a horse race or other sporting events, or mingled with the vibrant, vital people that filled King's world."

Their life was exciting, and their wedding was certainly different! Although Rae came from a place near Ottawa called Appleton, she then lived with her sister, Florence, and their widowed mother, Minnie, on Jackman Avenue in Toronto. Rae admitting she was "never in favour of lavish events" claimed that she "pressed for an intimate ceremony at 8:30 in the morning" at St. Joseph's Roman Catholic Church. The groom then had some very important business to attend to; he had promised to take his father to Hamilton for the football game, as the Ottawa Rough Riders were the visiting team. Only Clancy would attend a football game right after his wedding.

As it was just prior to the hockey season starting, and Smythe adamantly disapproved of players marrying during the season, they kept the marriage a secret. The honeymoon had to wait till Spring, when they went to New York. Similarly, Charlie Conacher was secretly married in August of 1931, but word leaked out in early November, so an announcement was then made.

Smythe's concern that a mid-season marriage was detrimental to a player's career certainly was disproved in Clancy's case. Most players do marry, even today, at the end of the season, but that is more for the convenience of going on a honeymoon and being together a bit before the groom must travel so much with the team.

It was less than two months after the event, and still unknown by the public or press, that Ted Reeve wrote:

> "King Clancy is probably, at this age, the most valuable man on the team with his play-making, his chatter, and his accidental tripping. Why he doesn't spend the largest part of the season in the penalty box for the way he pushes skates out from under puck carriers, or hangs onto them around the goal mouth, is more than we can figure out. But for all that, or maybe because of that, he is a mighty handy man to have around."

And so it was right back to work for the groom. One incident, which Red Horner well remembers, was the time Clancy imitated his boss in a dressing room pep talk. Smythe was noted for these. According to Horner, he would tell the team stories of some war hero he'd fought beside, how badly injured the man had been and what a tragedy it was; he'd almost have the boys in tears. Then he would turn the tone right around and tell how the poor fellow rallied, his fighting spirit came to the fore, and he single-handedly won the battle. Now the boys were ready to hit the ice and fight! Thinking Smythe was no where around, Clancy hopped up on a bench, clad in only a towel, and proceeded to mimic Smythe's gruff and raspy voice, telling some ridiculous war story he had invented. It turned out Smythe was at the door right behind him and witnessed the whole incident. But he had such a soft spot for his prize catch, he quickly forgave, and simply said to him, "All I want you to do is PLAY."

One of King's favourite stories is the night they tried to make Convey a star. Eddie Convey had been a good friend of Charlie Conacher's when both were Marlies, and he now played for the

New York Americans. Conacher, Clancy and Chabot sympathized with the guy, as he had always been an outstanding goal scorer until he hit the N.H.L., where he just could not connect. So the three of them decided to give him — now the opposition — a little help.

"Look," Conacher told them, "if we get a few goals up, let's make it easy for Convey. Let's help him score a couple." King was a bit concerned initially, "Are you crazy? Let him score a goal? You know what the ol' man would say; he'd crucify us." Sure enough, the Leafs went ahead 4-0 in the first period, and "it didn't seem like a big deal, we used to beat the Americans for a past-time."

As Convey skated down the wing, Conacher let him through; as he hit the blue line, Clancy missed him on purpose; and as he shot at Chabot, the goalie didn't move a muscle, left him a clear opening, but he missed. Next try, Conacher faked a body check, Clancy tripped himself, and Chabot left a whole side open; Convey missed again. A conference was held in the dressing room with the three Leaf conspirators. They decided to give Cowboy one more try.

Clancy even had to take his own team member, Red Horner, out of the play, and Convey had a clear shot on the goalie, who planned a fall. The only trouble was, as he fell, the shot hit him right in the Adam's apple. Poor Chabot could barely gurgle, let alone speak, but managed to gag a few words for the culprits, "Any more of this and he'll kill me." Conacher agreed, "If he comes down the ice again, we'll cut his goddam leg off." And Clancy had been right about one thing, "Don't think we didn't get hell from Mr. Smythe for that."

It seemed Charlie was the co-conspirator, or the butt, in many Clancy pranks; but most times it was really Clancy who was the goat in Charlie's pranks. For all the nonsense, they were the closest of friends. Clancy was one of the founders of the Charlie Conacher Research Fund, which sponsors such money-raisers as an annual dinner, a hockey game at the Gardens with the Flying Fathers (making $250,000) and a Bob Hope concert, always managing to get everything donated so that every cent made goes to the charity.

"You couldn't ask for a finer person than Charlie, a hard-hitting hockey player, a great scorer. When you got into a tough game, you were glad to have him with you. He, to me, was the champeen (as Clancy calls it) right-winger in the N.H.L. I never started a fight Conacher couldn't finish for me. He'd come in, knock a fellow down, push me on top, and say, 'You won that one.'"

Baldy Cotton can think of one that Charlie missed. "Frank went into the corner with Harold Starr of the Montreal Maroons, yakking and muscling the way he used to. Starr was a wrestler in the summers. He threw down his stick and hauled Clancy up onto his shoulders and did one of those airplane spins they do in wrestling. Around, and around, and around, and then he let Clancy go and he fell into a little heap."

But on second thought, King claims he did win one fight on his own. "Eddie Shore was down on his knees, so I belted him."

There was also the time Clancy and Cotton conspired to get back at Charlie for a few of his shenanigans. As Cotton tells it, "The worst trick anybody every played on me was this same Clancy. I've forgotten why, but I was really hot at Conacher. Maybe it was the time he dangled me out the hotel window, or else the time he crushed what I thought was my new hat.

"Clancy was always mad at Conacher, so we agreed we'd join forces and kick the hell out of him. I rapped on his door and said we wanted to see him. Conacher opened the door, towering over me; I turned, and Clancy was gone. I yelled for him, and he peeked around a corner and said, 'Who me?' Conacher tapped me once on the head and slammed the door!"

As for the hat trick, unfortunately not a goal scoring one, Cotton prided himself in a new bowler hat he had purchased and treated it like a fragile ornament. On one of their train trips, he hung it on a hook and went to chat in another car. Clancy was prepared and had a cheap substitute, which he quickly switched for the good one. When Cotton returned and sat down, Conacher and Clancy began to kid him about his "stupid hat." They grabbed the one on the hook, one tried it on, then the other, and finally they tore the brim right off. Cotton was furious.

There was another occasion about which Cotton reminisced to Jim Proudfoot of the *Toronto Star*: "Charlie helped King with the best body check he ever threw. Howie Morenz was coming down the wing, hell for leather, and Conacher hit him. Morenz went straight up in the air and Clancy took two steps and caught him on the way down. Poor Howie crawled off the ice on his hands and knees."

Morenz was the player for whom Clancy had the greatest admiration and respect. Not disputing the abilities of the Orrs and Gretskys of later years, King still is of the opinion that Howie Morenz of the Montreal Canadiens was the greatest player ever to lace on a pair of skates. Clancy told Brian McFarlane, "Morenz was the best I ever played against; he could start on a dime and leave you a nickle change." He told Henry Roxborough, "He could adjust to any situation. He could barge between the defence, or he could poke a puck between your legs, then wheel around you and pick it up. His shot was just like a bullet; and he didn't fool around looking for an opening, he just let it go. One year he scored forty goals in forty-four games, which would more than compare in today's schedule."

Clancy recited one incident of their playing for Dean Robinson in his biography of Morenz, "We used to marvel at the way he used to come in on us. I said to him after he skated around me, 'Try again and I'll cut your head off.' And he said, 'I'll be right back.' He was too, and over again slipped around me with the greatest of ease and shot for a goal, then turned and said with a laugh, 'Well, what are you going to do about it?'" All King could answer was, "Nothing," as he realized "there didn't seem to be anything else to say."

The two players had much in common; they played almost coincident years but for opposing teams; they were both devoted family men; they were both the life of the party and the life of the team, always keeping the other members entertained. The year before Howie's tragic death (heart failure at age 34, likely caused by the devastation of learning he could never play again after a severely broken leg) was the year Clancy retired. At the time, Morenz said to Frank Selke, "Clancy quit, eh? I guess he was tired. I'm going to quit too, it's getting too tough."

But sadness is not Clancy's element. One time he and Charlie Conacher were en route to Muskoka for a summer banquet, and the big fellow starts teasing the little leprechaun that he's the better athlete of the two. Clancy figured that, as they are driving along the highway, he's quite safe to assert that he is actually the better tennis player. He wasn't as safe as he thought, for as soon as they arrived in Bracebridge, Charlie headed for the nearest hardware store, popped out with a couple of racquets and a tin of balls. They hardly drove two more blocks before he found a court, and as Clancy tells it, "The big lug proceeds to chase me all over the court, till my tongue's draggin' on the ground, from 2 p.m. until dark. I'm not about to give up, but Charlie won't be satisfied until he proves he can play tennis better than me, which I knew all the time anyway."

Conacher was also friendly with the Chief of Police and would sometimes employ him in his schemes. The two (Charlie and King) were out driving one day and Charlie was stopped for speeding. As the officer approached the car, Charlie began to berate him. King jabbed Charlie in the arm to tone it down. The swearing got worse, and Clancy was hitting him harder and harder in the arm; he was afraid they'd be arrested, even thrown in jail. But the more King hit, the more irate Charlie got with the policeman. Finally the officer walked away in disgust. It was not until much later that King learned this had been plotted just to scare him.

To try and be one up, Clancy called in his friend, and at the time fellow referee, Bill Chadwick. When Conacher was the coach in Chicago, he resided in a hotel. At a time when his girlfriend was there visiting him (later his second wife), the boys did a little shopping for her on Charlie's behalf. They ordered up bouquets of flowers, from Charlie, boxes of chocolates, from Charlie, and finally some flashy items from the jewellers, all charged to and supposedly sent by Charlie! There wasn't much Conacher could do about the flowers and the chocolates, but it certainly was not easy to convince her the jewels just had to go back!

One summer, Conacher took Clancy along on a very special fishing trip to the West Coast. The wealthy Calgarian, Max Bell, had a magnificent yacht in Vancouver. He asked Charlie to bring along some friends for a trip up the coast. As well as Clancy, Conacher took along a business associate of his, Norman Bosworth (by coincidence, now a director of Maple Leaf Gardens). He and Clancy had met only rarely before. Charlie wanted to embarrass King, as usual, so he told him Norm was without a doubt the most refined gentleman, with the most impeccable manners, he would ever likely meet, all of which is most certainly true. Conacher went on to say that Norm was also very particular about other people's manners, frowned terribly on any rowdiness, and generally made him out to be quite a prude, which most certainly he is not. Because this was a business group, it was very important that Clancy be on his best behaviour, that he not embarrass Conacher in any way. They all sat down to their first meal on this fully equipped ship, with the world's best china, crystal and silver. Clancy was quiet as a mouse. He never lifted a fork before Norm. Norm noticed his every move was being watched and thought, *this is not what I thought King Clancy was like. I thought he was much more fun and outgoing.* The entire evening went by as dull as can be imagined. It was not until the next day that both Bosworth and Clancy clued in to Charlie's trick of making them both look like fools.

Sailing up the coast brought them to another big social event. They were going to meet a prince who had bought an island previously belonging to Mr. Bell. The plan was to drop in, and again they chided King he must be on his best behaviour and observe all the proper protocol. They gave him a run through of what he should say and do, and were pretty convinced he had it all down pat. When he goes up to shake the prince's hand, what does Clancy say? "Hi, Prince, I had a dog called that once."

King's casual informality has not changed. In the fall of 1985, when meeting Ontario's new Lieutenant-Governor prior to the official opening of Maple Leaf Gardens, the directors were discussing the correct way to address His Honour. Not Clancy, he just shook the man's hand and said, "How you doin', Linc?"

Clancy often acted as Conacher's caddy for golf; rare for a

hockey player, King was never a golfer himself. In Kingston, during a round, Conacher drove the ball right into Lake Ontario. "Clancy, you're the caddy, now dive in and get it." There was no way he was going to do that, but he did venture over to the shoreline to see if he could see it. He promptly fell in, golf bag and all. He emerged without the ball, soaking wet and mad, but never-say-die King finished the game.

One of the finest tributes ever given an active player was tendered on March 17, 1934. Centre ice featured a shamrock with "King Clancy" printed inside it. There was a whole series of floats, each one pulled by a player; some of the opposition team even helped. Each float also contained a player. A top hat contained Baldy Cotton, a potato spud had four St. Michael's junior B's, there was a book for George Hainsworth, a pipe for Ken Doraty, a harp for Joe Primeau, and a boxing glove with Red Horner (As Clancy used to say about him, "When he hit you once in a game, that was enough to affect you from stem to gudgeon".).

Finally a shamrock appeared, but out stepped New York's Bill Cook. Then last, but not least, Hap Day pulled a throne with Ole King Clancy, "grand and white-bearded, in bright green robes and wearing a crown. As he reached centre ice the lights went out, and Conacher and Day removed the beard and crown as planned. They then smeared his face with black" — some claim this was soot, some say shoe polish, but Clancy claims it was lamp black. "Anyway it got into my eyes, ears and throat. And I scrubbed and scrubbed, but it took days to get it off." As the lights came on again, he was helped from his throne by Day and Conacher while the band played "When Irish Eyes Are Smiling."

The King was then joined at centre ice by his wife and his father, the original King. There had not been adequate advance notice for his mother to get back from the West Coast, where she was visiting relatives. The usual speeches were made, as befits such an occasion, and mementos given: red roses for Rae, a case of pipes for the senior Mr. Clancy, a cabinet of flat silver, a silver tea service and a grandfather clock, inscribed for the occasion (still sitting and working in his front hall).

"That was the worst game I ever played. I stunk the joint out. Then Lester Patrick of the Rangers, after the first period, requested me to remove the green uniform because his players were getting all mixed up."

The *Toronto Star* reports, "It was bad business having Clancy play the first 20 minutes in that Irish suit. He was so strange looking that his teammates couldn't find him out of the corner of their eye when the game waxed fast and furious. They passed him up and passed the puck elsewhere."

The game may have been lousy, but the year was great: marriage, a centre-ice testimonial, and ending the season in first place, followed by being voted to the First All-Star team. The only disappointment was losing out in the first round of the playoffs to Detroit.

In fact 1933-34 was probably the most outstanding of Clancy's career. A few newspapers had fun that year with his playmaking ability: "Clancy, who seems able to fill in any time and any place when most needed, even in a hand of bridge, was right in his element. The Ottawa Irishman was up, down, over and back, and around that ice like Old Mother Hubbard."

"Clancy again showed the customers why the $35,000 the Leafs expended for him wasn't ill spent. He was up and around and attending to his own business and butting into everybody elses'. And with it all, he just showed that little extra finish which makes him a Clancy and keeps him above the others, who are just defencemen."

In the thirties it was not the rule for the team in the N.H.L. which finished the season with the most points to be league champion. Rather, there were two divisions, American and Canadian (yet strangely enough the New York Americans were in the Canadian section); the leader of each division was required to play a series to determine number one. In 1935 the Leafs beat Boston to become the league champion, and Clancy was no small part of that, "playing his greatest game of the season. The King hit 'em and he hit 'em and then he got up. Sometimes when he hit 'em it looked as though he would never get up, but he certainly put on a good all round display between bounces." He was obviously remembering his father's advice.

Conn Smythe was an advocate of the theory that, when the team made the playoffs, they were best taken away to a "sort of training camp," an environment removed from both normal day-to-day problems on the homefront and long-lost cousins begging for tickets.

One year, the location was Syracuse, New York, this year it was Galt, where they had access to the mineral baths. The press build-up was very encouraging; the Leafs were sure to win. The result was somewhat less; the Montreal Maroons beat them three straight. Ted Reeve coined what has become too often a seasonal lament: "Comes Spring, and the Toronto Maple Leafs Are Out."

A big event in the Clancys' personal life that year was the birth of their first child, Carole Anne. It seems only justified that she was christened on St. Patrick's Day. An item in the news column noted that a reception followed at the Clancy house, 2 Hillholm Road. How times have changed. Today professional athletes, like any celebrities, are forced to keep their addresses and phone numbers confined to a limited few. In 1935 it could still be safely published in the paper.

An expression which became synonymous with the Leafs of that era was coined by Lester Patrick of the Rangers, "It is almost axiomatic that as the King goes, so go the Leafs." And the season of 1935-36 seemed to prove that out.

For Clancy, things did not start off well. To begin with, Baldy Cotton, a part of the team which had become like a cohesive family unit, was traded to the New York Americans. King was plagued on and off by a foot infection, which began at his ankle and at one point appeared to have led to blood poisoning. And the press was playing up a new Leaf motto: "Youth must be served." As the season progressed, Clancy's foot healed and the team improved. Just near the end, on March 25th, the press leaked a rumoured trade which rather shook things up. The players named were Horner, Day, Jackson, Finnegan and Hainsworth. No team was mentioned and nothing ever materialized.

The Leafs finished in second place and beat Boston in the quarter-final, New York Americans in the semi-final, but lost their chance for the Stanley Cup to Detroit. The Boston series prompted an excellent piece in Bunny Morganson's column: "The spirit of Clancy goes around and around. And he gets better each time out. While Father Time may catch up with Clancy, they never will stop that battling heart. The Ottawa Irisher is tops, ace high, or what have you when the going is toughest. He never stopped talking to his mates throughout the game. He yelled instructions to every man. After Boston scored the first goal the King encouraged the Leafs with 'Now is the time to really go to work on this so and so club.' It was Clancy who started the wild scoring display in the second period. He outbattled the all-star, Babe Siebert, right in front of his own net, shoved over about the whole Boston team before he got the puck and banged it into the enemy's net. How many times over a period of five years has Clancy started the Leafs on their way with a fighting spurt for the first goal? Check it up sometime and you will realize just how important Clancy is to the Toronto Maple Leaf hockey club."

One night when Foster Hewitt was broadcasting a radio game from the organ loft of the Detroit Olympia, Clancy was badly cut around the eye. He had to be carried from the ice and receive immediate medical attention. In intermission, the rumour circulated that he had lost his vision and would be forced to retire. Foster chose not to announce this news, although concerned himself as to such a likelihood. In the final period, Foster heard motion behind him and glanced around. Here was the wounded player, pale and wan, and breathless from the climb to the loft eighty-five feet above ice level. King had heard word of the rumour, made his way to the booth, and handed Foster a note: "Please assure my wife that I am walking around, and will be o.k."

This is consistent with the way Red Horner remembers Clancy as a player. "It was not just his fierce determination on the ice. But he was always getting everyone all fired up in the dressing room. He could always get a laugh. He would come walking in with a big cigar in this mouth, knowing full well that smoking was taboo in the dressing room. But with that impish grin he could get away with anything. We all knew Smythe favoured him over all the others, but we didn't mind, as we liked him too."

The year 1936 also saw a new installation at the Gardens. Smythe seemed to be, on many occasions, a man ahead of his time. One evening, at Madison Square Garden, he was watching as Horner was being stitched in the dressing room and was alarmed at the lack of sanitary conditions. He remembered when the Garden first opened, the owner "arranged for ambulances to be lined up out in front to impress naive new Yorkers with the game's maiming possibilities." There were always attending physicians at N.H.L. games, but the facilities were less than adequate; the patient on the dressing room rubbing table, lighting usually indifferent, and the equipment only what the doctor carried with him. Smythe vowed to change all that, beginning at home. The Gardens was soon equipped with a spotless white hospital room containing all the facilities and lighting necessary to perform almost anything, excluding major surgery. He then approached the N.H.L. Board of Governors, recommending the same in every arena, and eventually all followed suit.

By 1936, Clancy was the highest-paid defenceman. He had played on three Stanley Cup winners and had been named to the All-Star team four times. He showed up, as usual, in perfect condition for training camp, but missed some of his buddies. Cotton had gone the year before, now Hap Day had been traded over the summer to the New York Americans, and Joe Primeau had announced his retirement. He started off the season in his regular spot, but as Morenz had put it, "He must be tired."

He had discussed the possibility of retirement with Smythe at the end of the 1935-36 season, but was convinced that, at 33, he still had the legs. He came to his decision in Detroit and the announcement was made in New York on November 24, 1936. "I am leaving the game to the youngsters. I thought it was about time I got out, I've decided to hang up my skates."

The papers were full of it. All items agreed, hockey was the loser. Clancy had developed a close association with many of the sportswriters, and after making his announcement around midnight, he wandered into the hotel room of Andy Lytle and elaborated further. "I'm 33 in February, and I know I've lost that old speed, that mythical half yard athletes talk about. I saw it very clearly in Detroit [the previous game]. I knew I was to take a certain player [Eddie Goodfellow], yet I stood as though rooted and let him score.

"I've had sixteen years of hockey and I think I'm doing the right thing to lay down my stick before somebody tells me to. It comes to all of us. I think the smart guy is the one who senses it before being officially nudged."

Lytle then talked with Conn Smythe. "Clancy was going to retire last year, but felt he had another good season in his system, and so did we. Any man who has given as much to the game as Clancy should be given the ungrudging right to decide for himself such an important step. We also want to be sure his health doesn't suffer. He is the best player we ever had, and ends his career without a blemish.

"He will be the goodwill generalissimo and used to bolster the morale of the team, at home and on the road. I hardly need tell you that King was one of the gamest, hardest working players in the Big Time. We'll need him around for a long time yet, to inject that spark of fight when the going is toughest."

To the *Globe and Mail,* Smythe added, "I hate to see him not back of the blue line for us, but there was nothing I could do. He told me of his decision and I said it was entirely up to him. Clancy had given us six years of great hockey and I cannot complain of any action he takes."

Clancy followed, "No one influenced me in my decision. I realized I had just about reached the end of the rope and could do more for the club by pulling out and making room for a younger man. I know it seems strange, and I regret to leave the club at a time when it is at the bottom of the Canadian group, but I think when the team hits its real stride and gets back on the top, everyone will be grateful for the move I have made."

There was one request he did make, typically thoughtful of his family, his wife in particular. "I don't want anything in the papers about me retiring, even if you think it's news, until I've talked to my wife and wired my father in Ottawa."

He did manage to reach his wife in time and had Rae call

Tommy Munns of the *Globe*: "I've just been talking to King. It was a great surprise to me to learn that he had decided to quit hockey, but I'm glad he has come to that decision, King asked me to telephone you and tell you that the decision is definite." And what did she say to her husband on that phone call? "How soon will you be home?"

Munns ended his editorial with a quote from Frank Selke: "Clancy's coming to Toronto transformed a good Maple Leaf team, which had failed to make the playoffs in the previous season, into the most colourful and brilliant organization in the circuit... In all their successes, the influence of Clancy's presence was manifest."

The message to the senior King Clancy somehow got confused and the news did hit his father as a complete surprise. He had received a telegram from his son on the morning the news broke, but not really pointing toward retirement. "Team slow to strike, but think youngsters will help us finish on top. About myself with team, everything fine. Will call you tonight."

Clancy's loyalty and consideration were extended even to his fans. He composed a valedictory, to be printed in the papers for each N.H.L. city, which follows in full:

"With all my heart I want to thank the hockey fans of every city in the National Hockey League, the newspapermen and others, who gave my clubs and myself the grandest support during the 15 years I have been connected with the Big Time sport.

"If it had not been for this, neither myself nor the league would have survived five years; let alone fifteen. I had the good fortune to play for two fine clubs, Ottawa and Toronto, and I tried to give those clubs and the fans the best that was in me at all times.

"There is no cause for me to complain over my treatment, and I retire, hoping the fans, and everyone I have come in contact with in my career are satisfied I gave my all, to the spectators their money's worth, and the club owners full value for my services."

As Andy Lytle ended his column, "And so in this hotel room,

high above the roar of Broadway traffic, and while most of this part of our world slept, 'finis' was written to as brilliant a hockey career as we Canadians have yet known."

FROM A DIFFERENT ANGLE

The rest of the 1936-37 season proved hard for King. He did travel with the team, but for as involved a player as he had been, he would always want to be on the ice with them. His number "7" sweater was put aside in case he reconsidered. There was no way he wanted to change his mind and take a chance on going to the minors. When you've lived on steak, it's hard to get used to hamburger again.

It was not as if he was without a job. He was very involved with O'Leary Construction Company in Ottawa, and had been for some years. This was a company owned by two bachelor uncles, Pat and Mike O'Leary, his mother's brothers. As construction was primarily a summer job, it fell in perfectly with Clancy to work for them; his home and his family remained in Ottawa. Over time he bought into the firm, until eventually it was his, whereupon he changed the name slightly to O'Leary (1956) Limited.

In earlier summers he ran a concession stand at Britannia Park, an amusement area near Ottawa. In purchasing his hot dogs, he insisted upon selecting them himself with the butcher. It was a very hot, very rainy day when he arrived at the packers, soaking wet. In they went to the meat cooler, and had what he thought was a little chat. When they came out his wet clothes were now literally frozen stiff. He became delirious on the drive home yet somehow made it. The result was: a serious bout with pneumonia, the last rites, and finally, thanks to a new drug called penicillin, recovery. Apart from his initial attack of diabetes in 1970, that was the only serious illness he has experienced in his lifetime.

During his first summer of hockey retirement, he was approached again by an old friend, Tommy Gorman, now the general manager of the Montreal Maroons, as they were in need of a coach. Having witnessed the spark his mentor had as a player, Gorman felt Clancy could be what was needed to ignite his floundering team. Gorman had led them to a Stanley Cup in 1934-35, but he was busy with other Maroon interests now, and the team had been steadily slipping.

On September 25, 1937, King signed his contract, and on December 31st he resigned. Their track record in 18 starts had been only six wins, one tie and eleven losses. The team just never got untracked, and the King chose to walk before he was given the papers to do so. It was obviously not just he, the whole team folded at the end of the season. His resignation seemed to spur the players of the opposing teams — all of whom loved Clancy — to beat the Maroons into oblivion, at which they pretty much succeeded.

At the time, Clancy's comment to news reporters was as follows: "I did the best I could in my first attempt in this kind of job. There was nothing left for me to do when they told me they thought it advisable for Tommy, who knows the players better than I did and consequently knew better how to handle them, to try his hand at the bench again.

"I wish him and the players all the luck in the world. They're entitled to it. With a few breaks I think the team can make the playoffs, and I'd like to see them do it. They honestly tried their best for me, but that just wasn't enough. I'm not saying anything more now, maybe in two or three days I'll give my version of the story." He never did.

The sports editor of the *Toronto Globe*, Tommy Munns, described the situation:

> "Every losing team must have a goat, so the resignation of Frank Clancy as coach of the Montreal Maroons does not come as any great surprise. Clancy stepped into a rather hopeless task and a red hot situation. Usually the goat of a losing team is the goal-tender, deservedly or not. Maroons fastened on what they thought was a more con-

spicuous goat than a player, and capitalizing on the fact that Clancy had enjoyed no previous managerial experience, put the ticket on him. While the downfall of the Maroons was taking place, Clancy alone shouldered the blame, and it was typical of him that he didn't attempt to shift any of the load, either to the management or to the players.

"No matter how hard the Maroons try their road will be a rocky one. I imagine that if the players of other teams think Clancy was shown the exit too hurriedly, they'll be playing when they meet the Maroons, with a view to proving to the wide world that it wasn't Clancy's fault."

Fred Jackson on the *Toronto Star* used a similar approach: "The King Abdicates. When the team just cannot click, the coach or pilot is the fall guy. That is King Clancy today; the fall guy for the Montreal Maroons. While Clancy has officially resigned, it can be taken as read that the resignation was just a matter of course . . . the door was opened."

The night of his resignation he took the train home to Ottawa with no immediate plans for employment beyond a return to O'Leary Construction. Clancy is in the very enviable position that, since his first experience in the army, he has never once had to apply for a job; he has always been approached. Not many can say that. (But then not many are offered a ten-year contract at age 80!)

After the resignation, Frank Calder, then president of the N.H.L., contacted Clancy and suggested he be linesman for some Montreal home games, close commuter distance to his Ottawa home. Calder's intention was to hire him later as a referee.

This was the first season to have linesmen in the N.H.L., previously there were two referees. So Clancy asked Calder what being a linesman entailed. "Just call the off-sides." At $15 for the work and $15 more for travelling expenses, this was like found money. It did not interfere with his construction company work, as he did not have to leave home until 5 p.m. and he was back again by midnight. The uniform was easy: his own pants, shirt and tie, and the league provided a white V-neck sweater with an N.H.L. crest.

He finished the 1938 season first as a linesman and then in the playoffs as a standby referee who never did have to standin. Calder was still convinced Clancy would make an excellent referee, so he tried a new tactic. He hired him for the 1938-39 season as a linesman, let him have a few games at that, then told him immediately prior to game time he would act as referee on this occasion. "But I've never refereed a game in my life before." This didn't phase Calder, also a good friend of Clancy's. "When you were a player you used to referee lots of games. Furthermore, the money is better; you get $35 a game."

This was a scheme Calder regularly employed to prepare a referee for his first game. George Hayes began the same way, being told at the last minute to switch with his partner. In this way there was no nervousness before their rookie encounter with this aspect of officiating. He did a good job, for eleven years. He even enjoyed it. Not so for Rae. "My wife suffered when they booed. It never bothered me. I laughed at it."

Previous to this appointment, the closest he came to officiating was a discussion he had on the subject with Red Horner, who commented that "the trouble with the referees today is they take too much guff from the players. If I was a referee, I would have fellows like myself out of the game during the first five minutes." Clancy then added that he "would chase all the bad men at the first sign of roughness." Some of the other team members nearly fainted at such thoughts of discipline, when King admitted, "And Red, you and I would last about three minutes if we ever tried to call a game that way."

There are countless anecdotes surrounding his days of refereeing.

The N.H.L. office found him notorious for not keeping an expense account. Finally they had to contact Rae and have her explain it to her husband, telling her the only solution they could see was not to pay him at all until he filed some expenses; it was done immediately then. Rae had always handled the money matters, he gave her his pay cheque and never gave it another thought. He has never paid a bill in his life, his son-in-law looks after that and allocates his spending money.

Bill Chadwick was a referee those same years and explains

how that aspect of hockey is so changed. "At that time there were only three referees and six teams. You were dealing with a maximum of a hundred players. You were able to get to know the players, what they were like as people, how they played.

"Now that's impossible. Referees are not allowed to associate with the players off the ice. They don't really know them as individuals, and with thousands of travel miles to twenty different arenas, you don't see any one player that often. It is all much more mechanical to referee by the rule book, not by your head."

Chadwick made another point which substantiates the proof of Clancy being such a popular referee — an unheard of combination. "Clancy is one of the few referees who ever played professional hockey. Throughout the game he was aware of what the player was thinking, what he was trying to do, how and why; he'd been there himself."

Perhaps the best known one-liner came when he was about to drop the puck. King edged close to Babe Pratt and commented, "You big lug, I wish I was playing against you tonight." Pratt couldn't resist retorting, "Who says you aren't?"

Also in Maple Leaf Gardens was the occasion of the doctor along the boards who was constantly belittling Clancy. One game, he had heard enough, "I may make mistakes, but at least I don't bury mine." Never again was he razzed by said physician.

There was also a lady who loved to aggravate him. "Mr. Clancy, if you were my husband, I'd give you poison." To which he blithely replied, "Lady, if I were your husband, I'd take it."

Also in Toronto, he was along the boards when he felt a severe blow to his head. He turned around and saw a man with a small souvenir hockey stick, realized that to be the instrument of the attack, and gave him a good punch. No wonder there is glass now above the boards surrounding the ice. Only later did he realize the man was one of the wheelchair patrons to whom Smythe always provided rail seats. Clancy was so embarrassed he asked not to be given any Toronto games for a while. Later on, he was explaining the story to the same Babe Pratt, who made him feel much better about the whole incident. "I figure you were both on even ground, he is crippled and you are blind."

There were several other cities where Clancy seemed to encounter particular problems. One of these was Chicago. To enter or leave the stadium, the officials, and players had to walk through an exit above which fans were seated. One patron was a regular, right in the front row. He leaned over and goaded all the officials whenever they passed. This particular evening, at the end of the game, as Clancy was exiting to the usual barrage of foul language, he quietly took the puck in his hand and hurled it right at the guy. According to George Hayes, who was walking behind, Clancy could not have taken a better aim, as the puck flew right into the man's open mouth.

The best of all in Chicago was caused by a woman. As King jumped on the boards to get out of the way of the action, he felt a nasty prick in an uncomfortable place. He realized the lady had stuck a hat pin in his bottom, and he was livid, as well as sore. He stopped the play and left the ice. The Chicago player, skating in on goal when the whistle was blown, for no apparent reason that he could see, was equally upset. King demanded the woman be ejected. Bill Tobin, the Chicago general manager, was more concerned Chicago might have missed a goal. The crowd waited. Clancy had the pin for evidence and refused to carry on if the culprit was not removed from her seat. It took some persuasion on his part and made for a few minutes with a bewildered crowd and no action. Finally, Tobin relented, she was asked to leave, or change seats, and the referee returned, still slightly uncomfortable.

Even his former boss, Conn Smythe, made a few comments. "I'll never forget when St. Mike's were playing Ottawa in the Junior playoffs. Here was Clancy, over by the Ottawa bench advising them how to beat St. Mike's. At the minor level there was nobody better. When he came up to our club there were nights when I sometimes wondered whether he wasn't the world's worst!" For the most part, Smythe did insist "he was one of the best referees in the National Hockey League, without even bothering to read the rule book." Clancy still insists to the present-day Referee-In-Chief, Ian (Scotty) Morrison, that they should "throw away the rule book and referee with just common sense again."

Boston was another city noted for giving Clancy a rough time. I guess there were just not enough Irishmen to protect him.

Two of King's better recollections of Boston in 1948 are words from a certain gentleman "up in the gods, in peanut heaven. After we've all been marched to the ice, there's a second of silence before proceedings begin. It is just long enough for him to yell, 'When you're through with the national anthem, shoot Clancy.'" Another time, the same man called down, "hey Clancy, we have a town near here named after you." The referee paused, thinking maybe this time he was going to get a compliment. He should have known better, as the name soon followed: "Marblehead."

Part of Clancy's refereeing was complicated by the fact he still knew some of the participants. "I knew the ones I had to watch. Syl Apps, for instance, I never paid any attention to at all." Particularly interesting was a game between his beloved Maple Leafs, now coached by Hap Day, his good friend and former teammate, and the Chicago Black Hawks, coached by another good friend and former teammate, Charlie Conacher.

It is quite likely that as a referee he had more trouble with the coaches than he did with the players. Day called Clancy over to the bench for a few genial words. Then Conacher followed, but was not so genial. "I guess you're going to give us your usual lousy calls, you s.o.b." Never at a loss for words, the reply came, "You'll get what you deserve." It wasn't four seconds into play when a Chicago player was caught visibly high-sticking an opponent. Clancy called it. Conacher commented, "That's the worst damn refereeing I've seen in my life."

Clancy was noted for not handing out misconducts. He and Bill Chadwick each consider the other to have been the best referee ever, yet their styles were totally different. Chadwick was strict, where Clancy couldn't be. In his autobiography, Chadwick said, "When you went out to line a game in which Clancy was the referee, you never knew what was going to happen. He'd drop the puck and say: 'All right you bastards, any way you want to play, you play, and any way I want to call it, I'll call it.' But he'd call very few of them. He refereed games with common sense, the most important quality any official in any sport can possess." If the occasion came for a misconduct, when a player questioned the referee's heritage or told him to do something indecent, Clancy always followed the same principle: he would ask him to repeat it, the player rarely did, so he was rarely called. Another tactic, when they were sarcastic, was to just say to them, "You're not doing so hot yourself tonight." Usually they would just skate off to the penalty box in disgust.

"In all the time I refereed I called only one match penalty. That was the Jimmy Orlando – Gaye Stewart fight right in front of the penalty box. They went at each other with their sticks so I had to call a match."

In all his refereeing days there was only one incident in which he was seriously criticized by the press. It was during a Stanley Cup series between Toronto and Montreal. A Montreal sports editor for *Le Presse*, Paul Parizeau, printed a picture of Clancy in his Toronto Maple Leaf sweater with the caption underneath: "When is Clancy going to take off this uniform." Clancy was livid and wanted to tackle him immediately, but was informed Parizeau was a huge hulk of a man. It was not until the next season that they happened to chat. After the conversation, Clancy asked whomever he was with the name of the man he had just been talking to; he was informed it was Parizeau. Clancy was surprised, as he was not the huge hulk he had been told, but rather small in frame, and they had managed to get along quite well. King admitted, "He seems like a nice enough fellow, but if he ever prints that picture again . . . ."

Coaching

In July of 1949 Clancy signed a two-year contract with the National Hockey League containing a considerable bonus and the title of chief referee. Two weeks later, on the 9th of August, an announcement was made.

The Montreal Canadiens were going to operate a new franchise in the American Hockey League. Frank Selke was the general manager and he was able to persuade his old friend King Clancy to take on the coaching. It was a difficult job to ask anyone to coach a new team in an existing league, but Clancy was always eager for a challenge. It would be doubly trying, as it would mean being away from his family more. There were now four children — Carole Ann, Judy, Tommy and Terry — so it seemed better for them to remain in Ottawa until the position seemed secure, After all, there had already been one previous coaching attempt.

At the time of Clancy's appointment, Toronto sportswriter Jim Coleman wrote a column in the form of a letter to the mayor of Cincinnati, parts of which follow:

"Dear Mr. Mayor:

"It has been brought to the attention of the public that the team which will represent your city in the American Hockey League next winter will be coached by one Frank Clancy, a lantern-jawed gassoon from Ottawa. Mr. Clancy soon will be as famous a landmark as the seven hills upon which beautiful Cincinnati has been built.

"Professional hockey is a new sport to your citizens, and consequently they can't be expected to appreciate Clancy's pre-eminence in that sport. You've seen Frank Clancy once before, Mr. Mayor. When the Montreal Canadiens and their Dallas farm hands played an exhibition game last Spring to open your beautiful new Cincinnati Gardens, Clancy was the referee."

As Coleman continued, he made an astute observation as to why Clancy opted for the coaching appointment:

"That, however, was the role in which Clancy always was least happy. Mind you, he was a good referee, but he didn't like officiating. He took the job only because it permitted him to retain his contact with professional hockey.

"You see, Clancy is essentially a gregarious fellow. He loves the company of hockey players and all other persons connected with the game. When he became a referee he discovered that he wasn't supposed to be seen in the company of hockey players. This was a terrible blow to him, because under normal circumstances, Clancy always could be found holding up a potted palm tree in some hotel lobby while he told lies to three or four hockey players. The N.H.L. President broke Clancy's heart when he issued instructions to the effect that the referees weren't permitted to stay in the same hotels as the hockey players.

"Clancy was a competitor, Mr. Mayor, a real competitor. Was Clancy a great hockey player you might ask. Just about the greatest, Mr. Mayor. Clancy was great because of his inspirational leadership on the ice.

"It is that quality that we are hoping that he still retains when he takes over the job of coaching your Cincinnati hockey team. Maybe if he wears a uniform, and skates himself, when he's clumping up and down behind the bench, he'll get back into his old flaming moods.

"Cincinnati will take Clancy to its heart, Mr. Mayor. And it couldn't happen to a nicer fellow."

Of all his working experiences, it turns out that this time in Cincinnati was perhaps his least memorable. The team struggled with growing pains, but never really got out of the basement. Their coach's efforts were not unrewarded, however, as he was chosen the A.H.L. All-Star Coach. Until a team establishes itself as a cohesive unit, until they have been together long enough to form some tradition, they cannot help but struggle. We have seen this more recently when the original six N.H.L. teams admitted expansion clubs; those franchises suffered for many years, but are now leaders of the pack. Under such circumstances it would be difficult to find a more suitable coach to ignite a little flame with some of his own spontaneous combustion.

His term in Cincinnati came to the simplest of all conclusions: it just ran out. Its first two years, the team existed as the farm club of the Montreal Canadiens, but the New York Rangers had shared a working agreement with them. The Rangers had their own farm team in New Haven, but they were suffering staggering losses. In 1951 New York decided to take over the Cincinnati team in full, and Frank Selke agreed that was advantageous to all concerned. It was presumed the Rangers would appoint their own coach, which they did, Clint Smith.

Frank Selke, a governor of the A.H.L., already had another job offer for Clancy, a dual post of referee-in-chief and public relations man for that league. "King will get more money in this job, and he'll have far less worry. The league feels it is wasting his talents by keeping Clancy in one spot. He'd do a terrific job of selling hockey around the circuit. He's just the kind of man we need. The public relations post is the one we want to emphasize."

Clancy did not accept as readily as usual; he took time to give it consideration. He had given up referee-in-chief of the N.H.L. two years previously and now he was offered the same position in a minor league. The compensation for this was two interesting add-ons, the public relations aspect and more money. He knew though that he would miss being part of the action again.

As was fortunately the case for him in such situations, the pieces just fell into place. Conn Smythe, at about the same time, mid-June of 1951, asked if he would take over as coach of Toronto's A.H.L. team, the Pittsburgh Hornets. Any connection to his beloved Maple Leafs was too good to resist. Here he would have a chance to groom the future members of the parent club and, who knows, maybe himself as well. This was one offer he could not turn down.

Clancy's superior talents as player were the same assets he brought with him to coaching: his unfailing determination, his fighting spirit, and his indomitable zest. One of his greatest teachers was Conn Smythe, and Smythe instilled in him the benefit derived from a rousing pep talk; both men excelled at this.

Some of the players he coached those two years in Pittsburgh have become very familiar names in hockey. On Clancy's 50th birthday, in 1953, the team beat Syracuse 8-1 and one of the goal scorers was Johnny McLellan, later coach of the Leafs. On the same team were such greats as George Armstrong and Tim Horton.

Playing for the Cleveland Barons was Johnny Bower, and his memories of Pittsburgh are not particularly fond. During the pre-game warm-ups the organist would play a song they had selected as their theme, "Lower The Boom, Clancy." King would stand on his team's bench, barking orders, and poor Bower would "literally shake in my boots with every note." He is convinced today that the music was an added inspiration to the Hornets. Somehow Bower rose to the occasion, and Cleveland beat Pittsburgh to the Calder Cup of 1953 in overtime of the seventh game. King credits Bower for winning that series, for "lowering the boom on Clancy."

The Pittsburg venture was more than successful. The team won their first game under their new coach and continued to win for seven straight more. By season's end they had clinched the league title, the first time ever for that city. Then it was on to Calder Cup play, where they eliminated the Hershey Bears in the semi-final and battled the Providence Reds 3-2 to take the trophy in 1952. The winning goal of that game was scored by Bob Hannigan in the second period of overtime. The newspaper headline read: "Thanks to Hannigan, Clancy Lowers The Boom."

The hero worship resulting from Pittsburgh's first-ever winning hockey team led to a great welcome at the train station when they returned from Rhode Island, and a civic reception followed.

At the final game of the Calder Cup series, a year later, when the team lost out to Cleveland, Rae Clancy and their two daughters were there. Judy well remembers that, in spite of the loss, the euphoria outweighed the disappointment. The fans still gave the team a great reception, and Clancy received an important phone call. It was from Conn Smythe, wanting to know if he would be available to coach the Maple Leafs next season. To go home to where his heart was, what more could a man ask for?

Before leaving Pittsburgh, he was given one more accolade, the Dapper Dan Award. It was not, as it would sound, for the best-dressed man in town, it was presented annually to the one who does the most for sports in that city, and he was the first hockey person in Pittsburgh to receive it.

On August 21st King Clancy was introduced to the Toronto press as the new coach. It was billed as the day he signed his contract, but his contracts with Smythe involved a handshake only; they were never signed.

"My job will be to direct the team from behind the bench and get them in a winning mood. If anything goes wrong, don't ask me about it. Go to them [Smythe and A.G.M. Hap Day]. They're running the club. And I promise you, if things get really tough, you won't see me at all. They tell me that I'm directly under Mr. Day. So when you come to me with your questions, I'll tell you to see Hap. He'll tell you to see Conn, and he'll just tell you.

"As a coach, I'm pleading with you now. I'm a rookie. But we'll have a good team. I've got a big guy from Cleveland [Bob Bailey] who takes a front seat for roughness. I'm counting on him squaring a few accounts for me left over from refereeing days."

Coaching for the Leafs meant that for the first time he could have his family with him. They kept the house in Ottawa, on Piccadily, and rented one in North Toronto. He would have to return to the nation's capital anyway, to continue his work with O'Leary in the off-season. The children were all enrolled in Toronto schools and got to see their father a bit more often.

It was on to the big time. And a success he made of that too. At the time, the Detroit Red Wings were the team to beat and the Montreal Canadiens were enjoying their Richard years. Nonetheless, Clancy's team placed third in 1953-54 and 1954-55 but dropped to fourth the following year.

Bobby Hewitson, sports editor of the now defunct *Toronto Telegram*, made some worthy comments at the end of King's freshman year:

> "This team, with Francis 'King' Clancy as coach, for the first time gave pleasing entertainment since last October. The pleasures of the campaign were many. There was the Irish humour touch that Clancy added from behind the bench; his in between games statements and quotes; his ready wit."

He went on with a little more optimism than proved true:

> "They were a green team in many spots during the past season, but with play and contact against better opponents, the greeness ripened closer to manhood for some of them: still room to go for a few. They are coming along when some of the stars of the other teams may be fading. The thing is, the building is being solidified, the weak spots found. And if the material is around to plug those spots, the Stanley Cup may be nearer than the fans and the Leaf management believes."

Just prior to the end of that first season, in early March 1954, there was a startling announcement made. The Leafs were going to play in Russia. A cable was sent by the chairman of the board of the Gardens to the Soviet ambassador in Ottawa:

> "The Toronto Maple Leaf Hockey Club is prepared to play Russian hockey teams in Moscow. Particularly Moscow Dynamos. Who have recently won the world championship. Early in May. Games against Soviet teams would be part of a European tour to promote international goodwill and would give U.S.S.R. an opportunity to see Canadian hockey at its best. Soviet Union would be under no obligation for expenses of the Toronto team."

The catalyst behind this wire was believed to be a game played the week before in the world hockey championships. The Canadian Amateur Hockey Association sent over a Senior

B club, the East York Lyndhursts, who were soundly walloped by the Moscow Dynamos 7-2.

A committee was quickly organized of prominent sports-minded Torontonians to raise some money to send over a professional team, and the Leafs were the obvious choice. Mr. Robert Saunders, a member of the committee and chairman of Ontario Hydro, expressed the opinion that "I think all of Europe would be interested to see how a top-grade Canadian team plays hockey. All they ever hear is that we left the best teams at home." Mayor Allan Lamport added, "A tour by the Leafs could clear up a lot of false impressions about Canadian hockey."

The players were willing to go along, but most expressed concern that they would not be paid, merely given travelling expenses and pocket money. Most worked in the summer, with salaries still being no where comparable to today's, and a Russian series would reduce their extra work time by about a month. Tod Sloan commented that he "would never go to Russia alone, but would be happy to have a chance to see the Soviet as a member of a hockey team." His wife, having two young children at the time, viewed it from another angle: "It's a wonderful chance for Tod to see the country, but I'd sure hate to see him away like that with no money coming in."

Right-winger Eric Nesterenko was of Ukranian background, so was by far the most enthused and also the most well-versed on the type of trip to expect:

"It would certainly put the whole light of the world on hockey and on Canada. And if the Russians gave us an unrestrained hand to look around as we please, the trip would give us a wonderful insight into the Russian way of life. I have a pretty good idea of things behind the Iron Curtain from talking to people who came out of there. But I would like to see it for myself so I can tell people in Canada from personal experience. I imagine the Russians will let us see only what they want us to see."

And what about the coach; the team could not very well go without him. "It would definitely do a lot for Canadian prestige."

After all this build-up to a great series, whatever happened? The *Toronto Telegram* headline of March 9, 1954, summed it up:"NO ICE, NO DICE, RUSS GAME IS OFF." There was no artificial ice yet in Moscow and any outdoor rink would have melted into a pond by the time the team could get over there, likely early in May. Was Clancy disappointed with this outcome? Apparently not. He was preparing to return to Ottawa and his job with O'Leary, so "I couldn't make the trip unless Russia is seven miles or less from Ottawa."

On St. Patrick's Day of that year, the King was the subject of what has become almost an annual newspaper feature. It began with "his day" in 1934 and has continued on and off since then, until now it would not seem like March 17th if the mighty leprechaun was not somewhere paid tribute to. For Toronto, that date will always seem like King Clancy Day.

In 1954 it provided for some jocular bantering between he and his boss, Smythe. On August 21st of the previous year, at the press announcement of his new job, he had promised that the "Maple Leafs will finish One, Two or Three in the National Hockey League. If we don't finish at least third, I'll go for a kick in the pants." A few weeks later, Smythe gave his seasonal prediction: "Leafs will finish fifth, behind Detroit, Montreal, Boston and Chicago, in that order."

Now, on March 17th the Leafs are in the playoffs, contenders for third place, the team has improved in all departments, and the goalie, Harry Lumley, is Vezina Trophy material. What does Smythe have to say now? It was, of course, just his way of needling Clancy and his players to get them going. Now he can say his prodding worked.

Clancy and Smythe always had a good rapport. Back when Clancy was one of his players, he teased the boss in training camp that a team consisting of Hainsworth in goal, the KID line, Hap Day and himself on defence could beat any N.H.L. combination Smythe could put together. Smythe agreed to prove it and would bet him $500 on the outcome. Clancy's reply? "I'm not a horse owner, I only play hockey."

Not to be overlooked in Clancy's success as coach in his initiation year was his assistant general manager, Hap Day. The previous year, Day had been in close touch with Clancy in Pittsburgh, in Toronto he could observe even more closely. As Bobby Hewitson put it, "The veteran defence pair, who helped Leafs to a Stanley Cup in the 1930's, who helped build the great fan interest at Maple Leaf Gardens, have stood side by side in improving a Leaf team."

The playoffs belonged to Detroit, it was the year when Gordie Howe and Ted Lindsay were the stars of hockey. Prior to the third game of the series, a crank had phoned two Toronto newspapers, threatening, "Don't worry about Howe and Lindsay tonight. I'm going to shoot them." It had an advantageous effect on their team, who won 5-4. Terrible Ted's reaction had been, "If I ever wanted to get two or three goals in my whole life, this was the night. That threat was the stupidest thing I ever heard of, but it made me mad." It must have; he scored a legitimate hat trick (three consecutive goals).

Howe's reaction was similar, although good for only one goal. "I personally couldn't have cared less what some crackpot threatened, but it annoyed me when my seventy-year-old mother got upset after hearing it on the radio in Saskatoon. The club placed a call to her so I could calm her myself, but I was still annoyed with the trouble the lunatic caused with his threat."

Bob Hesketh, now a radio sports commentator, had a little fun with his newspaper column, not so much with the threat as with the Leaf's position after the game:

Clancy at the Bat, or How Now Lindsay"

The outlook isn't brilliant for the Leafie team today
The score stands three to nil, with but one game left to play
And when the last time out they missed a fleeting grab at fame
A sickly silence fell upon the patrons of the game.

They thought the Wings might vanish
They even might at that
It would still be even money
With Clancy at the bat.

Maybe that inspired them, for they went on to win the fourth game, only to loose the series in the fifth. It was still a positive end to a season where the owner didn't even expect to be in the playoffs.

The 1954-55 season was almost a carbon copy of the year before. At season's end Clancy debated whether to go for a third season, but the prospects looked good. Some of his Pittsburgh stars were his stars once more, such as Army and Horton, and some great new rookies were coming along. Dick Duff, as one of those, remembers Clancy as being "a concerned and sensitive coach, always keen to your situation." They nicknamed the coach Delaney. Every time he made a player move on the ice, he would yell "Delaney"; but there was no such person, so finally they tagged the name to him. Throughout his coaching career his approach was always the same: "emphasize the positive, downplay the negative."

In later years, Duffy and Clancy continued a good friendship and today share an office. When Dick ran (unsuccessfully) for a federal election in a Northern Ontario riding, Clancy was out there stomping the beat and shaking hands with the citizens of Cobalt, New Liskeard and Kirkland Lake.

He took the 1955-56 season only to have the team slip a notch down to fourth place. He was even fined $200 for berating his good friend Bill Chadwick, who refereed a game in the playoffs. On March 30, 1956, the team lost out to Detroit 3-1 in the semi-final series. That was his last game as Toronto Maple Leaf coach.

Jim Vipond commented in his column in the *Globe*: "In Clancy, the Toronto organization had one of the most enthusiastic men to graduate from the player ranks. If there was to be criticism of King's work, it was that his spontaneous enthusiasm for the game sometimes made him forget such mundane things as line changes."

On April 2nd it was announced he was moving up to assistant general manager under Hap Day, now the G.M. He looked at it as "a concession to my digestive system. I'm tickled to death to get out from behind that bench. I was going to quit at the end of this season anyway. I haven't been able to eat or sleep for weeks. Coaching is the roughest job in the world. It's worse than refereeing."

His new post would also involve public relations and speaking engagements, a job at which he was a natural. At a banquet in Vancouver once, he preceded Bob Hope. His response was so great that when Hope took to the podium, his opening comment was "How do you follow that?"

His coaching job was still up for grabs, with three prime candidates: Turk Broda, Marlborough coach, Alf Pike, Winnipeg Warriors Coach, and Howie Meeker, who took over from Clancy in Pittsburgh. Smythe chose to follow a successful trend and upgrade his Pittsburgh coach, as he had done with Joe Primeau and then Clancy.

Smythe used some little tricks with both Primeau and Clancy to summon their attention. With Joe, it was a red light by the players' bench. When the light came on, it meant the Major wished to speak to his coach on a direct line. One day, Primeau, normally the calm gentleman, became so enraged he smashed the red bulb.

When Clancy came along, Smythe devised a more fail-safe system. King was, as he describes it, "wired from head to toe." He began coaching with a walkie-talkie which could not be shut off. When he found that to be exasperating, he would shove it away, and the crowd behind could still hear Smythe's gravel voice half smothered in Clancy's pocket. Aware of this, Smythe had wires taped to Clancy to give him electric shocks when it was urgent he listen. The Major could never sit back and let the coach run his own show.

Meeker was an astute judge of hockey and a good teacher, but the little Irishman with his unbridled enthusiasm was a hard act to follow. The team continued to slide, and with full deference to Meeker, it should be mentioned they were a team with an inordinate number of rookies. But the chips were down, and Smythe, Day and Clancy wanted a winner. So the mantle fell next year to Billy Reay. With no better success, a change was in the works.

King as an Ottawa Senator — Courtesy of Hockey Hall of Fame

Clancy's first team championship (he is far left in centre row)

Top Hat and Tails 1934

First ever All-Star Game Honouring Ace Bailey – February 14th, 1934

Back Row: Bobby Hewitson, Bill O'Brian, Hec Kilrea, Eddie Shore, Charlie Conacher, Bill Cook, Charlie Sands, Lionel Conacher, Andy Blair, Allan Shields, Baldy Cotton, Nels Stewart, Busher Jackson, Ching Johnson, Tim Daly, Mike Rodden.

Centre Row: Frank Selke, Red Dutton, Hap Day, Hooley Smith, Leo Dandurand, Lester Patrick, Frank Calder, Conn Smythe, Dick Irvin, Howie Morenz, King Clancy, Jim Ward.

Front Row: George Hainsworth, Ken Doraty, Larry Aurie, Bill Thom, Normie Hymes, Alex Levinsky, Frank Finnegan, Red Horner, Buzz Boll, Herb Lewis, Joe Primeau, Aurel Joliat, Charlie Gardiner.

Always the centre of action, even as a referee
— Courtesy of Hockey Hall of Fame

With his referee's whistle in the uniform of that era

After a successful year as coach — Courtesy of Hockey Hall of Fame

Coaching the Big Team – front left is Ted Kennedy

– Courtesy of Hockey Hall of Fame

1957 – with "his boys" – Terry on left, Tommy on right

– Courtesy of Hockey Hall of Fame

1957 – with "his girls", from left: Carole Anne, Judy and Rae

– Courtesy of Hockey Hall of Fame

With Frank Selke, and an ever present cigarette

– Courtesy of Hockey Hall of Fame

King and Conn Smythe — Canada Wide/Toronto Sun

1964 City Hall steps. Clancy on left – players visible to right: Ron Stewart, Allan Stanley, (stick boy Terry Clancy), Bob Pulford, Carl Brewer, Johnny Bower, Larry Hillman, Billy Harris.   – *Toronto Telegram Collection – York University Archives*

1964 Stanley Cup City Hall Reception. From left: Clancy, Imlach and Ballard as Tim Daly signs the book with Mayor Philip Givens, behind him, future Mayor William Dennison.

– *Toronto Telegram Collection – York University Archives*

Stepping Out – Punch and Clancy

The coach and his assistant in consultation.
— Toronto Telegram Collection – York University Archives

A Coaching Series — 1967

City Hall Reception, 1967. From left: Clancy, Tim Horton, John Bower, Larry Hillman, Dave Keon, Mayor William Dennison.

— *Toronto Telegram Collection – York University Archives*

Ron Ellis and Johnny Bower help King cool off after winning the '67 Stanley Cup — Canada Wide/Toronto Sun

Joking on exercycle with Johnny Wayne.
– *Toronto Telegram Collection – York University Archives*

A clean bill of health, 1967 — Canada Wide/Toronto Sun

King and friend Jim Gregory — Canada Wide/Toronto Sun

Opening game 1972 – being presented with the J.P. Bickell Trophy by Paul McNamara, Q.C. (Chairman of the Board)
— Courtesy of Hockey Hall of Fame

Jake Dunlap and Johnny Wayne pay tribute to King at testimonial dinner, 1975

– Canada Wide/Toronto Sun

King blows out the candles at centre ice

– Canada Wide/Toronto Sun

In 1975 some of the old guard gathered to pay tribute to their friend King Clancy. Clockwise from King are: Alex Levinsky,

Fred Robertson, Frank Finnigan, Ace Bailey, Harold Cotton, Harold Darragh, Hap Day, Joe Primeau and Frank Boucher

– Canada Wide/Toronto Sun

The boss gives King a new ten year no cut contract, 1983

– Canada Wide/Toronto Sun

The President and Vice-President of the Hamilton Tiger Cat Football Club

PUNCH

It was apparent some drastic move would be necessary to pull the previous champion Toronto Maple Leafs out of the cellar. Toronto was not, and is not, a city which is supportive of a loser. To begin with, there was a changing of hands in the upper deck. Conn Smythe was preparing to hand over the reins to his son Stafford. But it seemed he could never quite let Stafford alone to function in his own way, there was always some parental interference. This situation dogged the younger Smythe until his death. Stafford's right-hand man and closest friend in taking over the operations was Harold Ballard, and the feeling between Ballard and the senior Smythe was not exactly one of mutual admiration.

Stafford and Ballard were in Quebec for the annual June meetings and both had discussions with George "Punch" Imlach as to his feelings about coming to Toronto, but with no mention as to what capacity his position would be. He expressed willingness all right, but as he was under contract to Springfield at the time, a Boston property, he could not talk freely.

Apparently there was some discussion in Toronto as well, and one person to be consulted was King Clancy. Punch had barely met Clancy previously, but he did remember from seeing him play how well he could carry the puck up the ice, something he always admired, as it was very unusual for a defenceman. As assistant general manager of the team, how did Clancy feel about having a partner A.G.M., namely Punch Imlach? Punch had been told he could not be accepted unless Clancy approved. So what was Clancy's opinion of the idea? He felt he didn't really know the man, having only met him a few times in social gatherings, "but whatever you say is fine by me." The first formal meeting took place in Clancy's office on August 1, 1958, the day Imlach reported for work. That meeting led to what Imlach calls "the closest relationship I can ever remember having to anybody."

They began the season as partners, and Billy Reay remained as coach and shared an office with Imlach. It had been established when Punch was hired that he must be able to get along with Reay, and he supposed he could. And he did. It turned out, though, that Clancy did not. There was one other, more drastic problem; the team was still losing.

On November 21st, by his own urging, Imlach was promoted to general manager to give him a better control of the situation. The team continued to lose. Finally, in early December, after getting permission from Conn Smythe, Punch gave Reay his walking papers and took over the role of coach himself, giving him double responsibilities, and ultimately, a heart condition. One astute sportswriter commented that the way Imlach was getting promotions, while the team was continuing to lose, he might eventually get to be club president.

The Punch and Clancy combination proved to be a winning one, also one of the most celebrated teams in hockey history. As their prize defenceman, Allan Stanley, describes it:

"I never saw two people operate so well together, better than any married couple. Imlach made the decisions, that's why Clancy was always smiling; you can't be the decision maker, do the hiring and firing, and always wear a smile too. Primarily, Clancy was the buffer. He was the buffer with the players, with the management, and important too, the buffer with the press."

Allan Stanley was the second acquisition Imlach made after coming to Toronto. When many thought Stanley should retire, Imlach did not. The point was more than proven when Allan played ten great seasons in Toronto and another one in Philadelphia before finally hanging up his skates. Looking back now, he might have just as easily retired after the Leafs, but the Philadelphia stint served to leave him with one outstanding impression: "The high class of the Toronto Maple Leaf organization, the facilities in the dressing room, the whole attitude toward the players just cannot be compared. Toronto was A-1."

The very first player Imlach signed was Johnny Bower, considered another also-ran, who starred with the Leafs for thirteen years. One of Johnny's fondest recollections of the duo was at contract signing time. He was in Imlach's office and unaware that Clancy could overhear the conversation. After some haggling back and forth, they could not come to terms. A voice from the next office calls over, "What's the problem in there?" Imlach replies, "He wants a thousand dollars more than I'm willing to pay him." Clancy tried to soft peddle a bit, "I think he's worth it, so why don't you give it to him?" Imlach was not going to budge, "If I give him another thousand, then I have to give Mahovlich another thousand, and then Keon and Armstrong the same, and there's no way for that." Clancy closed the deal, "Then I'll give him the thousand myself, just sign it." Bower often wondered if Clancy ever did have to come forth with the money, as he was just the type to do so.

A similar problem occurred with Bob Pulford, now a general manager (of Chicago Black Hawks) himself. One September, he walked out of training camp when he and Imlach couldn't agree to terms. Clancy was called in, asked to return to Toronto, find Pully, and try and settle the issue. He caught up to Pully and asked what the problem was which had caused him to leave. In this case it was a paltry (by comparison) $500. Clancy agreed instantly to let him have it, provided he returned to camp immediately. "Pully was too good a player and too classy an individual, still is, to lose for the team."

One training camp in Peterborough, Johnny Bower arrived with his wife's lovely convertible. He knew that Punch had a friend in the car business there, a former football player, and it was a good place to have repairs done reasonably. Over lunch he mentioned that the car needed painting and asked advice. Punch told him to leave the keys in his mail box and he would see that it was taken care of, then Clancy arranged it all! A couple of days later, while the team was on the golf course, this car drove up. Johnny didn't even recognize it as his wife's. It was painted every colour of the rainbow — pink, orange, yellow, green, blue, red, purple, you name it and that colour was on it somewhere! He didn't know what to do, but he knew he certainly couldn't drive it. George Armstrong said he'd take it back to the hotel as long as Johnny came with him. It was a lovely sunny day, the top was down, and Johnny tried to hide while George gleefully pointed to his passenger and laughed as people kept staring at the wild car, and its occupants!

Finally, Bower waited until dark and decided to take the car back to his wife, let her solve the problem and retrieve his own car. He knew he'd have to miss curfew, which was a $200 fine, on top of whatever the new paint job would cost. But there was just no way he could be seen in that car. When he got home to a startled Nancy, she took one look at the car and made him drive it right back to Peterborough and have the culprits repaint it. The end result was that the dealer did a marvelous job, Johnny was never caught for missing curfew, and the total bill came to $50 plus gas!

Another player to come on the scene in the early days of Punch and Clancy was Red Kelly. He was not easy to come by, but proved worth every challenge. He had been a star defenceman with the Detroit Red Wings, on the First or Second All-Star team almost every year, was high scoring like Clancy, and a winner of the Norris Trophy for best defenceman in the N.H.L. and the Lady Byng for outstanding play with gentlemanly conduct (something at which he excels).

But by 1960, Kelly was disillusioned and Jack Adams decided to trade him to New York, where he refused to report. He preferred to retire as a Red Wing rather than play for another city.

While he was at home sitting it out, he received a phone call from King Clancy. "Would you consider playing for Toronto?" As Red puts it, "Who can say 'no' to Clancy for anything?" Furthermore, having been born and raised in the Simcoe area, barely one hundred miles from Toronto, he had grown up with Maple Leaf hockey on the radio, and the temptation was great. They agreed it was better to discuss things in person than over the phone, so he best come to Toronto. There was only one problem. Due to the colour of his hair, for which he is of course nicknamed, Kelly is instantly recognizable. It would be best if no one knew of any negotiations until something was settled.

Clancy called back and gave the message to Kelly's wife, Andra. He had arranged his air ticket under an assumed name and would meet him at the airport. In those days, it was not the big Pearson International, but a terminal in the town of Malton with an outdoor ramp from the plane visible to those waiting inside. King did not see the redhead get off the plane, so he figured maybe he'd never received the message, and turned to walk disappointedly away. He thought he would now have to return to the Gardens without his catch. Then someone tapped him on the shoulder, he turned around, and it was Red, wearing a fedora to maintain his disguise!

They drove down to the Gardens, slid in a back door and had their discussion. Adams had already agreed to the deal, giving Detroit Marc Reaume in exchange, provided Toronto could sign Red. Because he had been a leaf fan for all his early years, and really was not ready to retire, it did not take much to persuade Red to play. The next step was to notify the league, who had to record all player transactions before they were made public.

The deal completed, but still confidential, Red then went to the neighbouring Westbury Hotel and checked into the room reserved for him (still under the assumed name). While he was gone, King went to the phone. The call he placed was to Andra. He assured her that all was well, told her they had settled, and Red would play for Toronto the next night. There was just one thing he would like to know from her: which number she thought he might like to wear on his new team. Without a moment's hesitation, she requested, if possible, number 4.

Nothing was said to Red about the call, who talked to Andra himself later in the evening. Meantime the three (Kelly, Imlach and Clancy) headed out for dinner to celebrate. They decided upon Winstons, Toronto's most exclusive and elite restaurant at that time. As they walked from the parking lot, the same one used by many of the city's newspaper reporters, they passed Jim Vipond of the *Globe and Mail*. After all, the *Globe* office was right next door. But they were all trying to protect themselves from a driving snow, no one looked up and Vipond never noticed who the three people he was passing were; he missed his next day's story right there!

During dinner, a group of men arrived, the Montreal Canadien hockey team. Rocket Richard knew Kelly fairly well from All-Star games and such like, must have surmised the situation, but they confined their conversation to other subjects. A player never knows when he might be in the same position. Likely they all knew what was happening, but they also knew to say nothing. They would see for themselves when they played Toronto the next night.

The next morning Red arrived in the dressing room, and the secret was out. He had only packed a small bag, so it would not look as if he planned to stay; he was missing one thing though, his skates, he had only come to talk. Tommy Naylor, the trainer, had them flown in. When Red walked over to his spot in the dressing room, he was handed a sweater. As he looked at the number 4, he could not help but feel somehow King Clancy was the man responsible. As the years went on, they became close friends, Andra and Rae as well, and one of the Kelly children is nicknamed Clancy.

Player transactions do a lot toward building the team, and any that Punch made, Clancy was a part of. He was also a part of the greatest success their partnership created — three consecutive Stanley Cups. In April 1962, when they first achieved that ultimate pinnacle of hockey, the whole city of Toronto felt a part of it. A parade was held up Bay Street to the old City Hall steps, followed by a civic reception. There are varying estimates of from one hundred thousand to two hundred and fifty thousand people turning out to cheer the team and their dynamic coaching duo. Ticker tape was showered down from offices. It was an occasion none of them will ever forget.

Like a married couple, they were partners "in sickness and in health." In 1970, while on a road trip, King was not himself. He told Punch he really did not feel well and had little of his normal energy. Imlach, fearing it was heart trouble, wanted to get him to the hospital, but King would have none of that, he wanted to wait till he got home, and even then he was reluctant. When he was finally convinced he had to be admitted, it was discovered he had lost twenty-two pounds. "I had no idea what it was, and I was always afraid of that thing that got Charlie Conacher."

The doctor who detected the malady, diabetes, was Dr. Hugh Smythe, Conn's younger son, a very well respected physician, both in Canada and beyond. He soon put King on the road to recovery. He must now inject his thigh daily with insulin, monitor his blood regularly and control his sugar intake. He sneaks an ice cream on occasion, and his house is a haven for chocolate bars, which he keeps around for the grandchildren. His son Tommy well remembers when the candy and Cokes were a real habit with his dad, and marvels at how he can resist them as well as he does now. But with those three disciplines, and by giving up smoking, he can now keep his disease under control.

On Saturday, February 18, 1967, the shoe was on the other foot and a series of events occurred for which Clancy is probably best remembered today. The Leafs had been on a ten-game losing streak; it was a situation, even now, Imlach dislikes talking about. After the game-day practice, Punch sat on the end of the bench and said, "Gee, I feel lousy. I've got a congested feeling here," as he touched his chest, and moving to his left arm, "a lot of pain here." When Clancy suggested he see a doctor, his comment was "The hell with it. I got a hockey game tonight."

The two walked over to the Gardens commissary for lunch. While Imlach downed his customary two pots of tea, one of the team physicians, Dr. Tate McPhedran, came by leading a group of doctors on a tour of the Gardens. Clancy mentioned Imlach's complaints and McPhedran insisted he report to him at the Toronto General Hospital at 2:30. Clancy dropped Imlach over and then went home for his pre-game rest. (this habit is part of life for hockey players and coaches, and keeping quiet at that particular time is a vivid memory for all their families.)

At 5 p.m. Clancy received a call from Punch. "They got me locked up, will you run the club tonight?" The medical report was complete exhaustion caused by stress and requiring hospital rest. It likely would have led to a heart attack had he not been hospitalized then.

Clancy took over as coach, with no specific instructions, and beat the Boston Bruins 5-3. For the next eleven games, the team went on a winning streak and the newspapers had a field day. There was talk of bringing Joe Crozier up from the farm club if Imlach's hospital stay was extended. As Stafford Smythe, a man whom King claims he got along with very well, put it, "There will be no operating from remote control from a hospital bed and King Clancy will not be asked to take over the coaching duties. I wouldn't burden Clancy for long with these responsibilities after all he's done for us. It wouldn't be fair."

Clancy denied there was ever any interference from the hospital patient.

"Tell you why it's been easy for me to run this club. Imlach gave me carte blanche to do anything I want. I'm not afraid to make a mistake. When we started working together, it was understood I'd handle the club any time he needed me, but never full-time. This is Imlach's team, I don't take credit at all for what's happening. Don't believe that stuff about how they play better for me than for Punch. Any new guy coming in here would be a change for them. And some of the things I've done aren't new, it's just that Punch hadn't done them for a while. I'm not doing this job because I want to be coach. I'm doing it because he asked me to do it. You can't say anything to me about him; he's the fairest man in hockey."

Those are quotes taken from 1967, but if you were to ask King the same questions today, his answer would be almost a carbon copy.

Some of the players who had not been performing up to par now suddenly became stars. The team had not won in Detroit Olympia in over two years. Clancy decided to put in Terry Sawchuk, a former Detroit goalie who had been sidelined three months with a back ailment. Bower had been playing well up to now but had suffered a shoulder injury. Though not severe enough to force him out, he could stand a rest. The switch worked and Sawchuk "faced 40 shots and played as if he hadn't missed a game. He was more than great, he was super!" Clancy had been telling Imlach that if they brought back Sawchuk, and rotated the two goalies, they'd make the playoffs. Now they were at least on their way.

He also attributed the win to a little Irish superstition. "I told the boys there was no way we could lose. A bird christened my hat at 2 o'clock Thursday morning, after we got here, and Jim Gregory told me it was a good luck omen. The stain stays on the hat as long as things go well."

The success went on for ten games, with only one loss. The reasons were cause for great conjecture. Number One had to be Clancy. One player surmised, "Clancy has the ability to avoid creating additional tension in a very tense business." Ron Ellis, another player, was quoted, "He gets so enthusiastic in the dressing room that it has to rub off on the guys. He injects his own enthusiasm into us. And he gives everybody a chance, sends them out and roots for them. You have to play for a guy like that."

In almost any picture of Clancy coaching behind the bench, his hand is leaning on a player's shoulder; it could be any player, but that sign of warmth and affection is just one of the little things that help to spur them on. Allan Stanley also recalled an incident one year when they were in New York and the team had the night off to go to the Copacabana nightclub. Everyone had a few drinks, with the exception, of course, of Clancy. Yet who got up on the stage and had the whole audience in gales of laughter but King himself.

Players such as Frank Mahovlich and Mike Walton, who were both prone to nervous problems, suddenly shone forth. Imlach had no patience with such ailments, whereas Clancy did. When asked if he ever favoured any players, his reply was "always the ones who are down, the ones who need encouragement." Both these men were given more ice time and came up with more than worthwhile performances.

The concern then swung to Clancy's health. He was ordered to have a complete physical on March 1st. After all, he was sixty-four years old and coaching a hockey team in a city like Toronto was not the least stressful job for a man of any age, witness Imlach. The doctor's verdict, as told by King: "I'm suffering from numbpluck. That means I'm full of flapdoodle. 'A' — Number One, hundred percent."

Imlach finally recovered and returned to his post behind the bench. Unfortunately his first two games were losses, but after that everyone got used to each other again. Clancy's prediction: "We're going for the top of the heap. We may run out of games, but that's where we're going. We've got new motors on our skates and we're ready."

And they were ready. They made the playoffs and went on to win the Stanley Cup, and were the last Toronto team ever to do so. A group of sportswriters met and analysed what had happened. "The change had been a stimulant because of Clancy's bubbling personality. For nine years, many of the players had been seeing the same face and even the smallest change from routine was to be appreciated. Basically, Imlach and Clancy shared the same thinking on hockey. It was a product of the hundreds of nights they had sat together, replaying the game and plotting for the next one."

But as Allan Stanley said, "Clancy was the spark that won that Stanley Cup."

Clancy likely gave the best summation of his relationship to Punch in an interview he gave Bob Pennington in 1968:

"Let me tell you about Punch. Now there's one prince of a guy. I have never been closer to anyone. The guy has done so much for this club. So many people misunderstand the guy. They think he's tough and hard, when he's really soft and sentimental. His one weakness, if you like to put it that way, has been his intense loyalty to the Maple Leaf organization."

Through all this affection and loyalty, they did not always agree on matters. One of their bitterest disputes concerned Mike Walton, the same player Imlach had trouble dealing with and whom Clancy had made into star material. Now the positions were reversed. Shaky, as he was called, had skipped a road trip to Montreal. Rumour was that he was quitting. No one could seem to locate him. It took several days before the problem was resolved, and by then it had managed to involve Stafford Smythe (whose niece was married to Walton), Allan Eagleson, all of the sportswriters and the entire Leaf team. Walton finally reappeared and was ready to play, so Imlach dressed him for the next game, a 1-1 tie in which he, of course, scored the only Leaf goal!

Clancy was irate and remained so for days. There was, and is, one thing he just cannot tolerate and that is a quitter. King has always been a team man, always put the team first. He felt Mike was putting himself first.

The Mike Walton incident came to be one of the last in Punch's career with Toronto. He had not been able to develop a close relationship with Stafford Smythe, in spite of the Stanley Cups. Smythe had tasted champagne in the silver rose bowl for four years; he expected to do so every year. In the 1968-69 season, it was not certain they'd make the playoffs, then they did, only to be rapidly eliminated in the first round by Boston.

At this time, there was a hockey committee organized by Conn to be an intermediate group to span the gap between himself, Stafford and the team. At Christmas 1968, Stafford called an emergency meeting of this seven-member group (sometimes referred to as the Silver Seven) to discuss the fate of Punch. Stafford was for firing right away. The evidence indicated that Punch, although general manager and coach, would not listen to suggestions from Stafford or accept constructive criticisms on handling the team. However, Clancy, having been invited to attend the meeting by the committee, first stated his oft-repeated remark, "When Punch goes, I go." Aided by one member of the committee, that was enough to settle the issue.

Afterwards, at a press conference in the Hot Stove Lounge of the Gardens, Stafford explained that Punch was the general manager and coach, and would be until the matter was reviewed after the season. No one realized at the time that Stafford would make a sole judgement decision two minutes after the eliminating game with Boston. He walked into the coach's office and said, "You're fired," and walked out again.

A NEW ERA

"When Punch goes, I go." It became like an echo reverberating in Clancy's ear. Now Punch was gone, though not of his own accord, what would happen to Clancy, a man now sixty-six years of age? It first seemed likely Imlach would go to Vancouver, a team in the Western Hockey League, and one in which he had a considerable financial interest. Three thousand miles from home seemed a long way for Clancy. He told the *Telegram*, "I was a member of the first team that ever played here. I've been a part of this building since it opened. I played here and coached here and worked here."

The very night Imlach was asked to make his departure, Stafford Smythe took King aside in the first-aid room and asked if he would reconsider his former statement and stay on in an executive capacity. That night was not the night for an answer. Emotions ran high, to put it mildly, and it was a decision King considered "the most important of my life."

It took him two months to reach a verdict. With his family all in the Toronto area and his having been away from home so much, he based his decision on them. "I'm behind Punch one hundred percent and I always was. I did the best I could to help him. I should never have made that statement. No matter what I said, I'd never put hockey before my wife and family. It all came down to a decision between the Maple Leafs and Punch Imlach; it is as simple as that; if only it were simple."

Talking to sportswriter Paul Dulmage, he elaborated further, "Imlach is a high-class guy. We had a lot of good times and bad times together. We went through a lot. I know Punch will make his way wherever he is. But at my age, I wanted to stay where my family wanted me to stay. And to do that I had to abandon what I thought I might do.

"I don't think Punch understands that. Don't get me wrong. I wouldn't say anything to hurt Punch. But he's a lot younger than I am. At my age, you stay where you have roots."

Would he change that decision today if he could? Absolutely not. There was a time in the early stages when their relationship was somewhat strained. Punch did feel hurt then. Looking back now he realizes King made what was the right decision for him. Buffalo came into the picture for Punch and gave him a whole new chance. Their old friendship has returned intact, although they do not have the opportunity to see one another on as regular a basis. They each still speak of the other as the closest friend they ever had.

Several years later, Jim Proudfoot, a Toronto Sportswriter, reflected back on those days: "Clancy was devoted to Imlach, but leaving the Gardens would have been like leaving home or renouncing his Irish ancestry. When the time came, he just couldn't bring himself to go."

His new position at the Gardens brought him a new title, vice-president. He defines it as president in charge of vice. On other occasions he refers to himself as the big wheel that doesn't turn. Several years after his appointment by Stafford, Conn Smythe, the big wheel who first created the Gardens, asked, "King, what do you do around here now?" "Nothing, Mr. Smythe." His former boss advised, "Well keep doing it. You're doing a hell of a job."

For those first years, he acted as assistant to the new general manager, Jim Gregory, and the new coach, King's former Pittsburgh star, Johnny McLellan. He gave advice regarding players, made some scouting trips for them, and has always been involved in public relations for the team.

As Jim Gregory described their relationship, "It was like a family. In any family you cannot help but have some squabbles, fights or disagreements. Having worked for Maple Leaf Gardens for twenty-one years, often closely with Clancy, we had our disagreements. But like any family member, you still love them, and that's the way I still feel about King."

Most remembered of King's activities during the Gregory-McLellan era was his again substituting as coach, in 1972. As Frank Orr of the *Toronto Star* so aptly put it, "When he moves behind the bench to replace ailing coaches on an interim basis, Clancy's chief title seems to be winner."

King was again responsible for chauffering the coach to hospital and then replacing him behind the bench. And as per habit, the team also won. They had been in their predictable midwinter slump and as usual the goat was McLellan. Memories are short in the hockey world, as it was only the previous year he had been named Coach of the Year.

Johnny was a very warm and caring individual who kept his feelings inside; the result was an ulcer this particular time, and tragically, a few years later, very premature death from a heart attack. His friendship is still missed by any who knew him, not the least of whom are Jim Gregory and King Clancy.

As was usual for his sub-altern role, Clancy minimized his task: "My part in it has been overplayed. The club was ready to move when Johnny became ill. I talk to the coach every day. We discuss the injuries and the way players are performing. Once the game starts, there are moves I must make dictated by the way things are going. For the most part, I've just continued the way Johnny would have done them."

For his first game, the score was 2-0 in the Leafs' favour. His tally at the end of eleven games was six wins, three ties and who cares about the rest. A month later, a tanned and rested McLellan returned to the fray. Jim Gregory said at the time, "Johnny was worried that the strains of the job might be harmful to Clancy's health, even though Clancy has so much energy that its incredible and he had been bearing up remarkably well." Clancy's comment on that was "Heck, I'm the youngest sixty-nine-year-old running around loose."

The return was short-lived and McLellan had to admit the rigours of coaching were not for him. Clancy finished out the season by getting the team into the playoffs with three more wins out of a possible four. But still he downplayed his role. "It's a temporary thing. I do the best I can and when Johnny comes back [he never did] I'll return to my usual duties. I can stay a little loose when I don't have an entire season to face. It would be another matter entirely for a fellow with the whole season to think about."

The team finally went to defeat at the hands of the Boston Bruins in the first playoff round. One loyal Bruin fan, who for twenty-five years had carried on a verbal dual with Clancy every time the Leafs were in Beantown, had some sad comments to make after the game. "That was one game I hated to see Bruins win, because I think it will be the last time I'll see King Clancy back of the Leaf bench. At 69, this has to be his last year. He's really something, turned that team around and got them into the playoffs. He made tigers out of pussycats. I was surprised to see them give Bruins so much trouble in the five games it took to end this series. I was sure our guys would run the Leafs out of the Garden."

What comment did Clancy have to make about his old verbal sparring partner's lament? "I'll be back next season and the one after that if Leafs need an emergency coach."

The team directors that year chose Clancy as the winner of the J.P. Bickell Memorial Trophy, awarded to honour the first president of the Gardens. Its notation is that it be given to the team member who contributes the most in any one season. Clancy was the only non-player ever to be selected, but Ballard's answer to that was "He's a member of the team and the vote was unanimous."

Stan Obodiac, Maple Leaf Gardens' publicist at that time (and until his death in 1984), called it "Incredible. It takes King Clancy at age 69 to bridge the generation gap and reach those players."

Eddie Westfall, one of the classier members of the Boston Bruins team, took it a step further. "It's one thing to bridge a generation gap, but it's fantastic when you think he's jumping generations, not just one."

The Bickell trophy was only one item in a long list of honours accorded the King during his career: the Calder Cup, several Stanley Cups, All-Star teams, both as player and assistant coach, not to forget the Dapper Dan award. In 1958 it was election to the Hockey Fall of Fame.

It had been the dream and idea of Captain James Sutherland since 1943 to build a shrine in Kingston to the greats of hockey. When Sutherland died in 1955, the pictures and scrolls of the forty-two original selections were found under his bed. The N.H.L. finally appointed a nine-man selection committee and Harry Price of the Canadian National Exhibition in Toronto convinced them to place existing material in an administration building on the grounds, calling it the Hockey Hall of Fame.

To coincide with the reality of a location to house and display the memorabilia, the selection committee chose to make the list of honourees applicable to hockey up to that date, April 27, 1958. Among the list of 23 players was Toronto's King Clancy and his coach, Dick Irvin; among the 9 builders were two from Toronto, Conn Smythe and George McNamara (father of the present chairman of Maple Leaf Gardens, Paul McNamara). In 1961 this was all moved to a spanking new building adjoining the Sports Hall of Fame.

In 1975 a group of King's friends arranged a testimonial dinner. The recipient agreed on condition the occasion was made a fundraiser for his favourite charity, the Charlie Conacher Research Fund, specifically aimed at finding a cure for throat cancer. The dinner has become an annual event, now strictly honouring the cause, and has raised close to three million dollars over the years. One million dollars of this was recently given to the new research wing of the Toronto General Hospital, who in turn handed the decoration of the lobby over to the Conacher fund to do with as they pleased; included is a large mural of Charlie in his playing days.

The list of committee members of the Clancy dinner, and the Conacher fund, reads like a Who's Who of Canadian sport and includes his lifelong friend Harold Ballard, the present owner of Maple Leaf Gardens. In his invitation, Ballard began: "Francis Michael Clancy is just slightly older than Finian's Rainbow. Like most other leprechauns, he has never won a fight, on or off the ice. In more than fifty years on the Toronto scene, he has been a player, a referee, a coach and, most important, a friend of anyone he has ever met."

The date chosen was logically March 17th and the place had

to be the largest dining hall in the city (at that time), the Canadian Room of the Royal York Hotel. The dinner is still held there and is always a sell-out.

Ted Reeve, better known as The Moaner, recalled his first interview with Clancy when he came to Toronto from Ottawa: "Do you plan to play regularly with the Leafs?" The reply: "I guess so, Mr. Smythe's so poor we only got six sticks."

Punch Imlach chided him about being a notorious night hawk: "I think I got my heart attack staying up late with Clancy. After every game, he'd say, well Punchy, old chap, what's on the agenda?"

Johnny Wayne referred to him as the "B.J. Salming of the Stone Age," but allowed as to "hockey being our real culture, Clancy is the king of it. For fifty-four years, Francis Michael Clancy has contributed boundless enthusiasm, endless good humour, and great spirit to hockey and to the world. Who could give more?"

The Municipality of Metropolitan Toronto declared the date King Clancy Day.

Clancy is not comfortable as part of such tributes, but he loved this one, as he saw friends he had not seen in years. One of Conn Smythe's famous sayings was "Defeat does not rest easily on our shoulders." Praise does not rest easily on Clancy's. Now that he is not playing, refereeing or coaching, he never misses a sports page. Not so in his more active days. He read the paper meticulously, as his daughters remember, and never missed a crossword puzzle, but avoided that part of the sports page where he might have been mentioned. He did not want to know for fear it might affect his performance next game, be it playing, refereeing or coaching.

When before it was criticism he was avoiding, now it is the praise; he finds it embarrassing. He confesses that, aside from newspapers, he never reads, his main past-time is television. He is such an avid sports fan that at one time he had three sets in his family room so he could watch three games at once!

Of course, everyone thinks of King and the track. No one seems to know if he wins or looses; Dick Duff says he breaks even because he bets on every horse: "he gets tips from each trainer and would never offend anyone by betting one over the other." Milt Dunnell notices he always has his hands in his pockets: "I think he's saying his beads."

In 1982 he was at one of his favourite spots, the Los Angeles race track. A gentleman tapped Clancy on the shoulder and said, "Excuse me, but aren't you King Clancy?" "Yeah," was the reply, "I'm here with the Toronto Maple Leafs." Somewhat bewildered, the gentleman added, "Don't tell me you're still playing." This prompted sportswriter Rex McLeod to comment, "They would recognize the King if he were in Vladivostok for a holiday."

On February 24, 1982, he received a cable:

"It is not often that I have the opportunity to offer birthday wishes to living Canadian institutions and that is why I am so pleased to offer you my warmest greetings for this very special day. Canadian hockey without King Clancy would be like the Maple Leaf Gardens without Harold Ballard. Your outstanding career in the sport offers some hope to relative newcomers like Gordie Howe and Bobby Orr that they too can become truly great, if they will just stick with it. Please accept my very best wishes for a happy 80th birthday celebration. I hope that you will enjoy continued health and happiness.

Pierre Elliot Trudeau
Prime Minister of Canada"

How did he celebrate this momentous occasion? He left town. He flew to Florida for his annual holiday with his brother John, who lives just near Miami. That was his way of avoiding the many accolades, although he still returned home to a bundle of them.

Someone who has been around for all the joys and sorrows in Clancy's life for over fifty years is Harold Ballard. They met when the King came to Toronto from the Senators and Harold was around the Gardens as a young man himself, managing the National Sea Fleas (in spite of the name, they were a hockey team) and later the Marlboroughs. Their friendship intensified when King's beloved Rae died. Harold had experienced a similar trauma, losing his wife to the same dreaded cancer a few years previously.

King's children remember well and are most grateful for the way Harold took their father away from it all. As soon as they returned from the cemetery, Harold's car pulled up to the front door. He had an ice cream cone for each of them and tickets for a week in Las Vegas. The girls recollect seeing the two of them leave for their favourite place looking like a pair of kids. It was the break their dad needed and only Harold could do it for him. He continued to make all the road trips with Harold and the teams, Hamilton Tiger Cats as well as Toronto Maple Leafs, until the past few years, when his stamina has worn a little thin.

King has said of Harold, "He is a real true friend, true blue. He's done a lot of things for a lot of people. He's a real guy. No one will ever know all the things he does for people. Who would employ an old guy like me? That's what keeps me alive. This is what keeps me young: working with the young players and being around the kids." When King is asked when he plans to retire, his answer is always the same: "Never." He firmly believes that is why his father died relatively young; he retired too soon.

He still works with the young players too, but only if they ask. One who did so was Dave (Tiger) Williams, formerly with Toronto. When he was having difficulty with his shot, he went to visit King in his freshly decorated office. Nothing would solve the problem but a demonstration there on the spot. Clancy took a stick and aimed the puck — right through the wall. Jim Gregory was not exactly pleased, to put it mildly, with the King's treatment of the new walls or the puck which came flying into his office.

When Tiger was charged with assault after an infraction in a game (Ontario was in the process of trying to curb violence in hockey), Clancy attended every court session with him. On the day he was acquitted, his wife, Brenda, gave birth to their first child, a daughter, Clancy Williams.

Tiger says now, "Even though our ages are a hundred years apart, our philosophies are the same. He took me under his wing, and wherever I am or whatever I do, I never want to let him down."

All of hockey shares that sentiment. Long live the King, a rare jewel of a man.

BIBLIOGRAPHY

The Ottawa Citizen
The Toronto Mail and Empire
The Toronto Globe
The Toronto Telegram
The Toronto Star
The Montreal Star
The Toronto Sun

Chadwick, Bill. *The Big Whistle.* Hawthorn Books, 1974.
Coleman, Charles L. *The Trail of the Stanley Cup,* Vols. 1 and 2.
Houston, William. *Ballard.* Summerhill Press, 1984.
Imlach, Punch, with Scott Young. *Hockey is a Battle.* Toronto: Macmillan, 1969.
Imlach, Punch, with Scott Young. *Heaven and Hell in the NHL.* Toronto: McClelland and Stewart, 1983.
McFarlane, Brian. *Clancy — The King's Story.* Toronto: McGraw-Hill, 1968.
The Leafs — The First Fifty Years. Stan Obodiac, ed. Toronto: McClelland and Stewart.
Robinson, Dean. *Howie Morenz.* Erin, Ontario: The Boston Mills Press, 1982.
Roxborough, Henry. *The Stanley Cup Story.* Follett Publishing Co., 1964.
Williams, Tiger, with James Lawton. *Tiger — A Hockey Story.* Vancouver: Douglas and McIntyre, 1984.
Young, Scott. *If You Can't Beat 'Em in the Alley.* Toronto: McClelland and Stewart, 1981.

About the Author

Anne Logan is a Ryerson Radio and TV Arts graduate, and is now a freelance Toronto writer who has done work for such magazines as *Canada Century Home, Chimo, Flare, House and Home,* and the Maple Leafs' program.

Her father, Sydney Logan, whose biography she also wrote *(From Tent To Tower),* was a dedicated Toronto Maple Leaf fan. His close friendship with J.P. Bickell led to an association with Conn Smythe and resulted in Logan being elected to the board of directors of Maple Leaf Gardens from 1938 until his death in 1953.

Her father attended all home games and after each one returned home to awaken the baby and report on the outcome. As Anne grew older, even living in Vancouver for two years, her ardour for the Leafs never waned. At age 13, after a visit back to Toronto, she was boarding the plane with a prized possession, a teddy bear in a Leaf uniform. At the top of the ramp, the bear fell out of her hand and under the plane, presumably gone forever. In mid-air, the pilot strolled down the aisle clutching the missing bear and made a little girl very happy!

She later became a semi-regular attender of games and met Paul McNamara, part of the Leaf organization, and they married in 1976. Anne now lives in Toronto and summers in a 150-year-old schoolhouse, which inspired the topic of her next Boston Mills book, *School's Out,* a pictorial look at converted schools.